MW01221862

The Trailer Diaries:
How We Ran Away From Home

Rhona Davies

and

Anna Johnson

First edition copyright © 2012 Rhona Davies and Anna Johnson.

All rights reserved. No part of this publication may be reproduced, stored in a retrieval system, or transmitted in any form or by any means, electronic, mechanical, photocopying, recording or otherwise, without the prior written permission of the publisher.

ISBN-10: 1479360384

Published by Petrona Services Ltd.
rdavies1@shaw.ca

Printed by CreateSpace, North Charleston, U.S.A.

Printed in the U.S.A.

Acknowledgments

Maps pages v and vi : CIA World Factbook

Globe maps: Wikipedia, the free encyclopedia

Photo page 137 courtesy of
Richard Abbey at Lift&StorBEDS
http://storagebeds.com

Mojave phone booth photo: http://farm3.staticflickr.com

Thanks are extended to all the folks who encouraged us, and who gave us valuable advice, information, guidance, support and occasional rescue both on and off the highways and byways of North America and Australia.

Note: Some of the names of people in this book have been changed in order to protect their privacy. For similar reasons, Sunset Acres is not the real name of the trailer resort.

Dedication

This book is dedicated to all the risk-takers who heed and respond to the call of the nomad in themselves no matter what their age or stage of life, and to their faithful and sometimes long-suffering travel companions be they two or four-legged, especially to Smokey the Zen cat whose wisdom surpasses all things, and to the memory of Sooty.

Contents

"The world is a book and those who do not travel read only one page."
Saint Augustine.

THE JOURNEYS

MAP 1

Vancouver – Mesa - Vancouver:

5300 kms

THE JOURNEYS

MAP 2

Melbourne – Meekatharra:

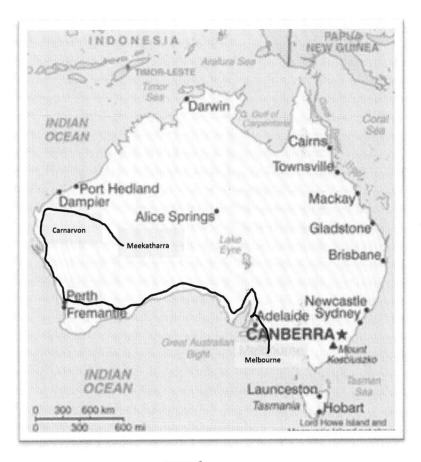

6500 kms

INTRODUCTION :

What Happened??

The fact is, nobody is really quite sure - what happened that is. One minute everyone was settled in your traditional, solid-foundation type of house; careers or retirement were chugging along in a steady, predictable routine kind of way; we could well have been considered a severely normal family, leading perfectly normal middle-class lives.

Next minute we were buying temporary dwellings on wheels, with huge reductions in square footage, and considering career or lifestyle changes that could possibly include opportunities to appear as "trailer trash" on a show like Jerry Springer's, but without the screaming and fighting.

When one of us chucked in everything to become a motorhome nomad, it at first prompted other members of the family to question her sanity. But then we started thinking maybe she was onto something. Maybe it was a sane response to the crazy, consumer-mad, thumb-texting capitalistic society that seems on its way to becoming the global norm.

On reflection, I suppose that for some people who have taken the major nomadic step of emigrating to a new land, moving on again from time to time is not as big a deal as it might be for those who opt to remain in one place and put down roots, anchoring their family ship in a safe, familiar home port.

As immigrants ourselves, living in one place for more than twelve years tends to makes us restless. That's a long stint for us. Since emigrating from Britain to Canada more than fifty years ago we have lived and worked in many places across Canada, and for two years committed ourselves to working in the Gaza Strip, teaching Palestinian students.

With the Gaza project it was the kind of situation where we said we'd sit down and carefully consider the pros and cons of taking such a major step, and then found ourselves wondering how we'd feel twenty years on if we turned down the opportunity. The thought of sitting in rocking chairs by the fire in our dotage, regretting what might have been, was so unbearable that we scrunched up the Pros and Cons list, chucked it in the waste basket and signed on.

Aside from any sense of adventure, we felt some degree of commitment to Canada for the benefits we had enjoyed as immigrants and citizens. Helping deliver an education programme that had been requested by a leader in a community struggling against cultural and political obstacles seemed as good a way as any of paying back and hopefully promoting the good name of our nation. We never regretted our decision. The warmth and generosity of people, and the rich cultural and historical antiquity of the region enhanced our lives far beyond what any tourist experience could ever deliver, and remain with us today.

It was on our return from the Middle East that my daughter Anna, though Canadian born, had decided Australia was the place offering the kind of future she wanted to be part of at that time. In response to my anguished hand-wringing and asking "Why?" she had the ultimate come-back: "But Mum – what were YOU doing when you were my age? Emigrating – right?" Right. Game, set and match. Futile to argue.

Some three years later her brother and his wife followed in her footsteps to the land of kangaroos and koalas. Later still, the youngest of the grown siblings left to live in the United States – practically on my doorstep compared to the Land of Oz. A five-hour drive south for a visit seems as nothing compared to an endlessly long international flight that leaves you staggering off the plane semi-conscious and incoherent, jabbering like an idiot from lack of sleep, Restless Leg Syndrome, and airline food. But we do it – family is family, and virtual visits on Skype are no match for the real hugs - and tears of course - at the airport.

The Trailer Diaries then, are two journals in one. They describe the more daring and adventurous travels of the younger generation – Anna's - and those of the older generation – the one Peter and I belong to now - whose travels, while less dramatic, represent the increasing unwillingness of senior citizens to take this aging business "lying down", so to speak.

Wherever we went we were part of the cadre of what Anna refers to as "grey nomads", eating up the tarmac, heading for warmth and sunshine. The driving and decision-making kept us mentally alert. Wherever we stopped for the night we tried to catch Alex Trebek's Jeopardy programme on tv, our traditional daily mental workout! Got to keep the old brain cells in good shape.

The Diaries are also about two wonderful continents – North America and Australia – that are now home to me and my children and that seem to share much in common. They are young countries with a Can Do attitude as opposed to the "Ooh, you can't do that; who do you think you are?" mantras that are often the legacy of the culture Peter and I opted to leave - European monarchies with their entrenched class systems even when most of the nobility have been demoted to so-called ordinary citizenship. Riding bicycles and mingling occasionally with the "working classes" (i.e. the folks who do the really hard work to keep the country running) do not fool anybody who has lived in a true democracy where your accent, place of birth or father's occupation are mere items of

3

curiosity, not designators of your status on some archaic, traditional, social ladder bent on destroying whatever dregs of self-esteem you have managed to hang onto.

While a visit to a monarchy might be nothing more than a tourist exercise in curiosity and quaintness, living there long-term as a subject of the monarch is vastly different from the sense of personal power and dignity enjoyed by a citizen of a country free of such antiquated notions. It is the significant distinction between the Old and New Worlds – the one holding you to tradition and the past, the other beckoning you to freedom and the future.

I made my choice long ago, with no regrets – just the occasional nightmare where I wake up in the darkness disoriented, panic-stricken that my life in North America was just a wishful dream! And although Australia is much older geologically, and, like its North American counterpart has a long-established and acknowledged aboriginal settlement in its history, its present-day governance and ethos are essentially "new world."

There are enormous land areas on these two continents that at first glance appear similar. Landscapes with colours, features and geology each reminding you of the other, though on closer interaction with them the differences in flora, fauna and climate become evident.

The red earth and rocks, and sage green shrubbery of the southwestern United States are highly reminiscent of the Australian Outback. Shown a random selection of pictures, at a cursory glance each could be mistaken for the other. In both there are the vast blue skies, mind-numbing distances on highways that seem to disappear into infinity; long periods of drought followed by raging floods; ghost towns; poisonous insects and reptiles; the desert canines - coyote and dingo; the ability to quickly lose any sense of direction and distance in a hypnotic, endless landscape.

They are powerful and awe-inspiring components of both continents; they leave you thinking that maybe, in the grand scheme of things, nothing really matters – a missed deadline, a lost lottery ticket, the latest cell phone – except for human kindness and an appreciation of how interconnected all living things are.

The Diaries are a record of the travels, adventures and experiences that led to significant changes in our perceptions of just how much stuff and space we humans really need as we leave our inevitable footprints on planet Earth. They are not intended as preachy environmental messages – even beavers use up their environment and move on; at least two of us are still carnivores; we LOVE big-box hardware stores, indoor plumbing and flat-screen colour high definition tv's. But we're trying to do it all with a bit less of an impact. It's not going to save the planet (there are simply too many of us now) – NASA has to find us a new one of those to go and inhabit – and most likely trash – but we sleep a bit easier at night, and *we can see the stars*!

Rhona Davies.
West Coast of Canada.
September 2012

A Note About The Diaries

 Indicates that the section is written by the Canadian author (Rhona Davies, a.k.a. Mum)

 Indicates that the section is written by the Australian author (Anna Johnson, Rhona's daughter)

CHAPTER 1

February 2011: Vancouver - Melbourne

The Best-Laid Plans ....

We are scheduled to visit Anna, my daughter and oldest child, who lives in a pretty little house in Melbourne, Australia. We try to go Down Under every couple of years or so to catch up with her and Ben (my older son) who lives in Sydney. Both are Canadian born, but in the ever-changing world of job availability they found their different niches in Austral latitudes and have adopted their new citizenship with the same enthusiasm that I adopted mine on emigrating from Britain to Canada many decades ago.

We love staying at Anna's place. She has done wonderfully creative things with the house and garden. Walls and windows in the bungalow-style house open concertina-style onto a garden which she has transformed from a junky mess into an oasis of native plants, trees and a small pond. When she goes to work we look after the place, cook, keep it clean, feed Smokey and Sooty the cats, and Honey the dog, ride our bicycles into Williamstown to get groceries or catch the train into the city. Perfect. This is what we're expecting again. Everything is booked.

Then suddenly the plan is abandoned. Anna announces that she is quitting work. She's had it with the frenetic superficial world of media capitalism; had it with filming almost twenty-four hours non-stop at one shoot to keep company costs down; had it with not getting enough sleep, ordering food and snacks for prima donna film biz people who have no concept of waste and out-of-control indulgence; had it with a million limitless demands. Not that she ever fell short of meeting them. Her skills were legendary and in great demand. She has been paid well and looked after her finances. She intends to sell her pretty Melbourne home, buy and fix up an old motorhome, and take off into the Australian wild-blue-and-sand-coloured yonder with her faithful animal companions. She has money in the bank. She has skills. She won't go hungry.

The house sells in two days, but the old motorhome - newly christened Waggin' Trail - proves to be a bigger challenge. It takes more time than Anna had anticipated to get everything replaced and installed. The RV repair and reconstruction guys are appalled at the state of the ancient vehicle and say she should abandon it and get something much newer.

"You should dump it, luv. I'd be ashamed to take this heap out on the road."

But Anna is determined to get her bargain roadworthy and habitable. However, it is obviously not going to be a quick fix.

The Stunt House

So when we arrive for our scheduled visit, Anna is temporarily renting living space in The Stunt House, so named because it belongs to a friend who is an agent for stunt people who act in movies. It's an interesting place; we've never been this close to what's involved in making movies before, so we are fascinated and curious.

Anna generously gives up her rented bedroom for us, and sleeps on an Art Deco satin-upholstered chaise longue in the central living area of the house – it is a large house. The couch is a prop to be rented out for stage sets when needed. There are clothes racks with rows of costume outfits : hats, feather boas, old-fashioned dresses, men's jackets, lots of spangly accessories. Other pieces of stage furniture sit around the room.

At the far end is the kitchen which is shared by people who work in the stunt film industry and who also rent living space in the house. They all respect each others' food purchases in the fridge, and are generous at offering anything you find yourself short of when putting together a meal.

We meet Brent who makes a living throwing himself off rooftops and fast-moving vehicles. He gives us a mini lecture on how important it is to know how to break a fall when you land. We take notes since you never know when this might come in handy. Others in the house write the safety reports and instructions that tell dangermen and women like Brent exactly when to take what will look on-screen like a death-defying (or sometimes not) leap into certain oblivion. This is all new to us and makes social demands we are not accustomed to. How do you start a conversation with someone who takes the occasional broken collarbone and trip to the hospital as all part of a day's work? But we have to try.

"So what did you jump off today, Brent?"

"Aaah. Nothin' goin' today mates. Wind was pissin' around blowin' in all directions – too dangerous. We'll 'ave another go at 'er tomorrer."

We agree that our efforts at mastering a new conversational mode have been an unqualified success. Crikey!

The Makeover

Waggin' Trail gets a new hot water heater, roof-ladder, inside makeover and mechanical upgrades. At the rear is a double bed which Peter and I are to share when we all set out on the planned road trip. Anna will sleep on a folding cot outside the bus under the retractable awning, weather permitting. Right now she is giving the outside a full paint job with a sort of Mexican theme. Skulls decorate the side panels. Anna gets her friends to help, but their aesthetic goals outstrip their actual art skills, so Anna tells people it's a mural done by a local primary school group as a class project.

With Waggin' Trail's departure delayed, Anna generously moves us into a small apartment close to trains, buses, shops and terrific bicycle paths. If Waggin' Trail is ready in time we shall all three head off into the sunset for a two-week adventure on the road before we return to Canada.

Anna takes us for a couple of try-out bone-shaking local trips, but alas, Waggin' Trail needs even more tweaking than we old folks do, and it is with much sadness that we finally have to say Adios and wish Anna, Smokey, Sooty and Honey exciting but safe adventures when everything is ready for lift-off. We head back to Canada and await the adventures of Waggin' Trail with its captain and crew.

CHAPTER 2

April 2011: Melbourne - Adelaide

Homeless.

I was at the top of my field: a successful TV commercial production manager, staying in five star hotels, living the mortgage dream, eating stress for breakfast with an iPhone in one hand while scrolling through stock market day trade picks, popping Xanax like lollies in between constant cups of coffee and filterless cigarettes. Daily motto: "Bring it ON!" Then one day I was walking the dog on the beach, texting a crew for the next job and thinking about public liability insurance when I simply stopped in my tracks, looked out at the sea and said without thinking, "I quit."

So on April 1st, 2011, at the age of 48, I ran away from home, taking only a small, poorly-converted motorhome bus, two cats, a dog, an inflatable boat that I bought on the internet for $99.00, a folding bicycle, dog carrier, a record player, a guitar that I couldn't play, a hatbox, power tools and a box set of original series Star Trek DVD's. My plan: not to have a plan.

The Travel Companions in Waggin' Trail

| Honey | Smokey | Sooty |

The Bus

Friends and family were quietly horrified by my motorhome of choice: a 1986 Mazda T3500. It came with old solar panels, an inverter, shower, toilet, kitchen, plus, for no extra charge, spiders, rust and mice. Mum said "Why don't you get something like a nice Winnebago?" My theory was that since the bus cost only $16,000, the engine, gearbox and wheels could all fall off on the Nullarbor and towing and repairing it would still be cheaper than paying $100,000 for a schmancy grey-nomad-mobile, and then having THAT towed off the Nullarbor.

Also, the Mazda was so old and basic that it could be repaired by any passing farmer with wire and duct tape. My choice of a crappy old bus was vindicated many times on the road - I came across plenty of other travellers with nice new rigs broken down in the middle of nowhere, waiting for expensive parts, their travel budget blown to bits, while I puttered past, blowing a bit of smoke, duct tape wrapped around a busted fuel line.

The other advantage of buying an old bus was that the most interesting and rewarding parts of my travels were when things went wrong - that's when I met amazing people and got to know odd little towns that I would otherwise have just driven through with barely a glance.

I did plenty of research before I set out, and copied down the extensive lists of "things you must carry" in your motorhome when travelling in the outback......air compressor, tool kits, rescue kits, flares, valves, gasket-making tools - but I threw the list out when I realised that there would certainly be hundreds of wildly over-prepared retired guys who would be pleased as punch to tell me off for not carrying an arc welder and a complete set of imperial and metric socket wrenches , then get out all their toolboxes and say to their wives "I told you we needed all this stuff."

Nearly everyone asked me why didn't I just rent my house out, "just so you have something to come back to if you need it". But I wanted to throw myself in the deep end - if I was going to have an adventure, I was going to go whole hog and commit myself to living out of a bus and just seeing what happened. It turned out to be the best thing I ever did.

Day 1

On the road at last! Carefree, no schedule, nothing to do but check the tyre pressure, oil, water, fuel, trip meter, voltmeter, inverter, solar recharger, gas burner, gas barbecue, gas hot water, jerry cans, toilet chemicals, flush level, fuses, pets, fridge door lock, external hatch locks, vents, aerial in lock mode, drawer locks, kettle securely stored in sink, taps off, rear blinds tucked away, bike straps tight, solar party light panels in place, gas leak alert in "on" position, glow switch off, water pump on? or off? laptop strapped down, tv bolt in travel mode, dammit what's that annoying rattling noise at 93 km/h and did I double check both cats are in?

Terrified and excited, I set out from Hoppers Crossing in Melbourne as friends and family wave me off. The first big decision: turn right or left at the freeway? I head west, the direction of frontier myth, the vector of pioneering dreams; also the handiest off-ramp to the next McDonald's.

I rumble along the highway smiling and tapping my toes to my country western music. Inside I'm exhilarated and panicking. What have I done? Oh my god - I sold the house! Try not to think about it. Friends' phrases bounce around in my head: "Are you going to take a gun?" "Won't you get lonely, or bored?" "What about serial killers?"

Oblivious to my internal turmoil, Smokey clings to the edge of the desktop while Honey snoozes on the passenger seat. Sooty has buried herself under the doona in total denial; I feel like joining her. Oh my god I sold the house I sold the house...

I arrive in Apollo Bay. It's windy and cold. My imagined scenes of gaily chatting around an open fire and swapping tips on deep cycle batteries are left unfulfilled as everyone hides in their caravans to watch the news. I watch Star Trek and then lie awake trying not to think about the fact that I'M HOMELESS while listening to Smokey fight with campground resident cat Jasper in the bushes. I've carefully parked the bus at an awkward angle which makes me slide slowly headfirst down the bed into a neck-crick position against the window which, as the rain sets in, starts leaking.

Next morning, discreetly observed by the other motorhome campers who pretend they're not looking, I employ a basic thirty-seven point turn to un-park the bus which seems to have wedged itself among some trees and random posts that I don't remember seeing the night before. I smile and wave. Ha ha! I meant to park that way! I lose count of the number of raised eyebrows among the grey nomads emerging from the shower block as I creep past in my disgraceful-looking vehicle. Everyone seems to be wearing matching faux-Gortex His & Hers leisure shorts 'n' shirt combos.

Miraculously the bus makes it through the steep hills of the Otways. I stop for small excursions to waterfalls and other scenic sights, but the urge to drive west pushes me on. What does it mean, to be living on the road? Am I a tourist? Should I stop and look at everything, read visitor signs, collect brochures and take photos? Oh my God, I sold the house! I'm living in a bus! Don't think about it just keep driving.......coffee coffee coffee...... what's that noise? Is the bus breaking down? Oh my God I sold the house I sold the houuuuse.....

Reaching Port Fairy many hours later, I wander on a fruitless search for some mythical free camp paddock spot that a friendly ex-hippie told me he stayed in ten years ago. I check into another caravan park. My campsite neighbour is an older lady living in a tiny Hiace van. She sets out jars of water in order to "energize them with the natural balancing properties of the sun and the moon", then gives me two small shells as a gift, or possibly a hex.

Pets and Panic Attacks

Back on the road heading along the coastal highway. Pets settling into bus life. Honey sits next to me on her bed, Smokey rides shotgun on the desk behind the passenger seat and Sooty hides behind the shoe box next to the shower cabinet. They're all wearing locator beepers. Smokey knows when we're only stopping for a short break - he hops out, has a quick look around, then returns to his travelling spot on the desk. Much mirth from onlookers when he accompanies Honey and me on walks. Sooty is the one I worry about – she's a bit of a wild one, independent and not too thrilled about the confines of the bus.

My panicked internal monologue continues slightly less unabated. I try to focus on the positives – no debts, no mortgage, no bills, no job! The feeling of freedom is wonderful, but I also feel a bit anchorless – who am I now, without a job or a neighbourhood to define my place in the world? A good stiff drink of vodka seems to help (I have seven bottles under the bed – goodbye gifts from friends), and there's nothing like a good tidying up session to settle the mind - I decided to leave the Xanax behind in the big city where it belongs.

I decide to downsize some of the impulse camping purchases stuffed in every nook and cranny of the bus. Why do I have three fly swatters? I throw one of them out.

The west beckons; in my mind I am driving towards some vaguely imagined beachside free camp where there's internet, dolphins and balmy summer breezes. In the Real World rain is leaking in through the front windscreen.

Smokey Sees The Sea

Southend Beach Caravan Park, sort of northwest of Millicent in South Australia. Grassy site overlooking a gorgeous beach, sun is shining and hardly anyone there; I book in for a week. First test run of my home-made awning system (bits of matting, fencing and solar party lights from Bunnings) results in passersby coming up to ask if I'm running a market stall.

Smokey is fascinated and horrified by his first view of the ocean; overwhelmed, he heads off to hang around the toilet block. I let Sooty off her leash at last; she disappears into the bushes to wreak havoc on the local insects, of which there are a LOT.

Panic levels subside with red wine intake plus emails and phone calls with friends. Ha ha! Yes I'm having a ball! (ohmygodIsoldthehouse Isoldthehouse). I go exploring on my folding bicycle; Smokey tries to run along with Honey and me, then gives up and returns to his post at the toilet block.

Grey nomads arrive and celebrate their arrival at this peaceful seaside paradise by starting up their generator, then come over to check out my TV aerial. "We can only get 20 channels on ours, we don't know what's wrong with it." What with all the noise and hurly burly I only manage to get fourteen hours sleep.

It's a Hard Life ....

This is it. Living the dream. Day trading the stock market in pyjamas and a cowboy hat, Liberace on the record player, sand in the bed. Strolling along the beach with a glass of wine, the vast star-filled night brings out all the big questions. Who am I? Why am I? Did I turn off the gas?

HANDY RV TIPS

Here are a few handy tips that they don't tell you in the motorhomer manual:

- Earwigs are located in the laundry bag
- Combining antibiotics with cab sav on beach at night can cause nausea and identity crisis
- Check the water tap isn't salt water before filling drink bottle!

Testing the Waters

Today gets a 9 out of 10 (needs frolicking dolphins to get full 10) . . . long stroll on beach with pleasant retired gentleman, painting the bus, only one bloke asking questions about inverter; gentle breeze, sunshine, a quick swim (the water's great once you get out). Have started attracting local pets who are very interested in getting into the bus. Smokey ventured on to the beach during my swim and sat howling at the ocean - "WTF is that? I mean WHAT IS IT? Why are you IN it?"

Long serious conversation with grey nomads about who got what discount on the hot showers, culminating in elderly task force trooping off to the caravan park office to try to get another 5% off the 6-dollar a night site fee.

Have not worn shoes for three days!

Neighbours and Nature

DIVINE. Hot 'n' sunny, lots of swimming, a hike around the cape, could stay here for ages. Today's exciting RV action included changing a fuse. Relocated the bus to shelter from the morning wind, causing grey nomads at the other end of camp great consternation resulting in a long discussion about whether they should turn their bus around as well. Today's annex theme: Gilligan's island look with ramshackle bamboo fence and solar party lights. Giant flying insects crawling on laptop screen as I write. Next: The Coorong, then Adelaide and stockin' up at the mall.

Note to self: Remember to wear clothes!!

The Coorong and the Big Lobster

The Coorong is a stunning wetland wilderness, but how can it possibly compare with the breathtaking artistry of The Big Lobster? Sadly no actual lobster on the cafe menu but I console myself by purchasing my first motorhome fridge magnet.

Not sure what time it is as I think parts of the real world went on or off daylight saving time, so I believe you make a half hour adjustment ahead or behind for South Australia unless you're in dairy farm area or Smokey tells you it's dinner time in which case it's probably five o'clock.

Have I mentioned how totally excellent it is driving with your own toilet?

Landing in Adelaide

Cold and rainy in Adelaide, but weather mitigated by the pleasure of seeing my old friend James and his daughter Lucy. We meet Henry Cat and he and Honey instantly share massive flea infestation. A fun-filled Friday night with chemical baths and a zesty Shiraz.

It's calming to share a bit of family life and the simple pleasures of a fire, home cooking and familiar faces. My so-called courage in abandoning normal life to live in a bus is nothing compared to the journey James and Lucy have struggled through following the death of partner and mum Julie, and we sit outside in the garden, a little bit sad, a little bit happy, wondering where our paths will lead in the years to come, comforted by sharing our stories and thoughts.

The big issues of life are soon eclipsed by a sudden plan to check out the South Australian Museum's Giant Squid which, according to 11 year old insider knowledge, is awesome and measures 13 feet in length, not counting its two principal tentacles! That's an awful lot of calamari. But will there be a fridge magnet?

CHAPTER 3

December 2011 - January 2012:
Vancouver – Mesa

Friendly Persuasion

What are we getting ourselves into? We've never really shared our neighbours' enthusiasm for seniors' resorts in faraway places - refuges from our Canadian winter. It seems to be an aged citizens' version of Hit-and-Run : When the temperature drops to around 5º Celsius they hit the road and run to warmer climate zones.

Lots of older folks do the annual migratory pilgrimage to Florida or the American southwest, desperately seeking warmth and sunshine for the old bones and joints. Snowbirds, we call them in Canada. In Australia Anna calls them "grey nomads". They return in the spring, tanned and relaxed, while the rest of us cough and hack our way through the seasonal 'flu epidemic that seems impervious to the annual vaccine shots we endure.

We have always imagined these destinations to be sinister walled ghettos: protected, detached communities of overweight seniors who, behind electronic gates and under the ever-watchful eyes of closed circuit cameras, scoot around in motorized wheelchairs or worse still, golf carts. We are terror-stricken, not at the warnings of one of our sons about rattlesnakes and gila monsters in the Arizona deserts, but at the pictures on the internet of groups of party-hat-wearing, champagne-glass toting seniors determinedly having Fun. We have never fitted in with the golfing, card-playing, church-going, crowd – why should it be any different now? At least, that's what we're thinking.

The closest we have ever come to anything like this was when neighbours and acquaintances persuaded us, against what we felt to be our better judgement, to go on a cruise. Cruises sounded like the same kind of setup – floating ghettos with casinos and mind-bending amounts of food being consumed by people who should long ago have switched to grass and lettuce.

In the event, we cracked under pressure and booked a cruise through the Inside Passage of Georgia Strait, all the way north to Alaska, and we did indeed see marvels of nature up the Alaskan coast. Our misgivings were somewhat borne out though, by the fact that at one of the shore stops, of 1400 passengers on board ship, only four of us showed up for the wilderness hike with the totally authentic, Moses-bearded, staff-carrying, rubber-booted old outdoorsman who delivered one of the most informative nature experiences we have ever had.

Along with truly fascinating explanations of the evolution of lichens and mosses to grasses and plants, we came across Grizzly bear tracks and the hastily-abandoned remains of recently-killed salmon – presumably the bear or bears had fled at the sound of approaching humans. The outdoorsman had warned us of a possible encounter, and shown us what to do in terms of avoiding a knock-down-drag-out fight that would inevitably end up with the bear in the winner's circle. The final stretch of the nature expedition was comprised of a river-raft journey back down to the ocean, accompanied only by the sound of water lapping the sides of the inflatable dinghy and the cry of Bald Eagles overhead.

To this day though, when people ask us if we enjoyed the cruise, we say we don't know. Some parts were good, others left us wondering about social issues like waste disposal from all these ships plying the ocean waters; gluttony and excess; disturbing scenes of crew members from the Far East scrambling to line up onshore to make a desperate call home from the one available public phone booth near the dock before the ship's horn announced imminent departure.

Later, we asked one of the waiters whom we'd seen in the lineup, if he had managed to connect with his family. "No this time," he said. "It was middle of night there, so I no get to talk to my little boy because he asleep. Maybe next time." Relative to what he could earn in his own country, the cruise ship work pays well, and he was working so that he could pay for his son to go to school and get a good education.

So we expect we may have to put our social consciences on hold again if we head south to the sun. With the world in its current turmoil, and the ever-diminishing number of safe places in which to spend down-time, we figure we'd better go and get it done now while we still can; worry about future scenarios the likes of The Hunger Games if or when they materialize.

In Australia, Anna's adventures in Waggin' Trail have provided inspiration and self-reflection. She's been on the road for several months now, and although it hasn't always been easy-going, she loves it. Crises occur from time to time: flat tyres, fuel-line leakages, wrecked gear box – but she sees the positive in everything The Road throws at her and always seems to land on her feet; rescue is always to be found somewhere if you keep your wits about you (and have plenty of spare cash to throw at problems of course).

Our ventures into the realm of trailer living will be far less challenging. It would be the end of our 37 year relationship if Peter and I ever attempted anything as scary as trying to drive an RV of any size. Just parking such a vehicle would trigger either serious mental breakdown or heart attack! So we shall proceed with caution and try staying in a grounded vehicle that requires no driving - essentially a mobile home with its wheels coyly concealed by a "skirt", giving it a more permanent and cottage-like appearance.

A neighbour contacts somebody who knows somebody else, and before we know it we have delivered a cheque in US dollars to a couple of people in a nearby town in Canada who have recently purchased and renovated a mobile home in one of the Arizona seniors' resorts but are unable to use it due to health problems. Their winter home of sunshine is available for one month, and we think that should be just about a perfect amount of time for us to assess how much we can tolerate before we start screaming and heading panic-stricken back to Sky Harbor airport in Phoenix.

The whole trailer park scene is one to which we have never really given much thought. We'd see them around and assumed these are people who cannot afford full-on, built-from-the-ground-up houses constructed of wood, cement, brick and stone veneers, stucco, vinyl siding and such – "proper" houses. Trailer parks, we assumed, were for losers – people who can barely make it and who would really prefer to live in "proper" houses with all their attendant resource-draining mortgage burdens. From what we hear though, the seniors' mobile home resorts are a whole different ball-game.

Whatever. We reckon ourselves to be flexible, pretty adaptive people. We emigrated to a new country, have lived in several Canadian provinces to avail ourselves of jobs, worked for a government programme in the Middle East. So we'll go and spend a month living like high-end trailer trash; the experience and humiliation will be good for our souls – we keep telling ourselves we need new experiences, so better get on with it. Worst comes to the worst, we'll catch up on a lot of reading.

Departure Day

Departure day arrives. We've packed minimal clothing; bare essentials for what we hope will be a warm climate, with a sweater for cool evenings. Activity gear takes up most of the space in the sports bag: tennis racquets, hiking boots, walking poles, binoculars for bird-watching. The e-book technology takes care of our reading needs – we try to keep techno-savvy when it makes some kind of sense. Coming from a generation that was educated to *think*, we don't need the constant, thumb-twitching entertainment of i-phones and i-pads. It's all we can manage to try and shut down our entertaining minds every night in order to fall asleep!

Time comes to head for the airport. In the courtyard we encounter Charlie from next door. He and his wife returned just a month ago from their first resort expedition; loved it so much they bought a unit right away and can't wait to go back. Charlie smiles and waves to us.

"'Bye!" he says. "You won't want to come back – you'll see!"

Yeah yeah, we think, as we return the neighbourly smile, wave, and head out to the airport…. *yeah yeah*.

Since it's mid-winter in our part of the world, we opt for flying to the land of seniors-only trailer resorts. Our neighbours drive down in late October before winter really gets going, and make the return journey in the spring to avoid snow and ice. They do it in two or three days, and say it's a piece of cake. But right now it is January and weather conditions on the roads and passes north to south are unpredictable. We have heard horror tales of motorists being caught in unexpected snow storms, hoping that whatever is the American equivalent of Canadian Tire will be within towing distance when they are extricated from a snow bank and have to purchase chains.

God only knows what we would do in such circumstances. It takes us all our courage just to check the car's tire pressure at the local gas station. Chains sound like advanced auto mechanics to us. We emigrated to Canada well past the age when most of the home-grown population would have learned about survival things like chains, jumper cables and towing hitches – the basics of driving in a vast country where people living in prairie provinces think nothing of driving fifty miles for a game of tennis or a movie. So – this time out, we are flying.

Airport Musings

As we sit in the departure lounge in Vancouver international airport, we are acutely aware that this seems to be a predominantly aged people's flight. Age-group-wise, we definitely fit in. However, our clothing definitely does not. Nobody else seems to be wearing hiking boots, zip-off pants, and shirts made of fabric that reputedly keeps you warm when cool and vice versa.

One of my layers is from the kind of active gear store that seasonally hires young guys who purport to be expert in tackling anything the outdoors throws at them, and who love to impress with their "coolness." I had stood looking at the labels on a shirt, struggling with words like 'breathability', 'wicking', 'climate control' (climate control?? Does it come with a thermostat or built-in weather balloon or something?).

"That's a great layer to wear next to your skin," said a voice belonging to someone who looked to be fresh out of Grade 10. "You can wear it for two months without needing to wash it."

I had nodded, trying not to look incredulous, inwardly thinking that the idea of not having to change or wash your personal laundry for two months must seem like paradise to guys of his age.

"Seriously," he added, for good measure, "Me and my mates wore this stuff when we climbed K2 a couple of years ago. You can't do laundry at those altitudes – it'll freeze." Oops – my mistake. He's probably all of 20 years old.

I bought the shirt because I liked it anyway regardless of its ability to suppress odour-producing microbes long enough to cause skunks to avoid you.

An elderly fellow plunks himself down on a seat in the airport waiting area, with a sigh of relief after walking from security to the waiting lounge – a distance of about 80 metres. A young woman sits facing him. She smiles and asks where he's off to.

"Mesa," he says. "Somebody pickin' me up at Phoenix airport and drivin' me to the resort. Goin' to be stayin' there a coupla months fer the warm weather."

"That's nice," the young woman says.

"Where ya from? Here?" asks the old guy.

"Yes," she replies, "I'm from Vancouver. What about you?"

"From Saskatoon. Saskatoon – that's the capital of Saskatchewan, ya know. Ever hear of it?"

"Of course I've heard of it," she says, "Everybody knows Saskatoon is the capital of Saskatchewan."

"How come ya know about Saskatoon if yer from here?" asks the old-timer.

Dear lord, I'm thinking, is this what we're in for? The young woman's voice is now just short of sounding a tad edgy as she hangs in and says, "I know about it because I went to school."

"Aw. Right. So you learned, like, geography and stuff like that then?"

"Yes, that's right," she says and manages a smile that we're sure must belie an urge to deliver a smack.

But it also sets us thinking how amazing it is to still run into people who, for whatever reasons, and like our own parents back in the old country, did not get much schooling. Maybe this old timer slogged away his youth and middle years helping to keep the family farm going, producing crops that Canada has been renowned for; crops that not only fed his own expansive country, but helped feed many others in the world that were less fortunate.

We remember gifts of food being delivered to our primary schools in England just after the war. The headmaster would call an assembly for the whole school and we'd all troop in, awestruck to see boxes of apples - the labels clearly telling us they were from British Columbia - set out on tables at the front of the assembly hall. The boxes would be carefully opened, and the paper-wrapped apples (such a treat after war-time rationing) distributed in quiet, respectful awe while the headmaster told us about the generosity and kindness of the Canadian people.

British Columbia – back in class we had to find it on a map. To us it could just as well have been Shangri-La, it looked so far away and sounded so exotic. If anyone had told us then that one day it would be our home we would have thought they were mad. We hardly knew of anywhere much beyond the "dark Satanic mills" of Blake's poetry which pretty much summed up our own industrial city.

So maybe this old-timer at the airport came from a family who had sent food to Britain. For its time, his knowledge of fields, seeds and planting, harvesting and storing grain, would have been the parameters of a different kind of education. The country needed people with a different skill set from today's demands for new, rapid learning and global awareness. We wonder if he's going to be one of our neighbours at the same resort. If he is, it's going to be interesting.

In any case, it's boarding time. We join the line of elderly snowbirds and shuffle our way to the gate, trying to fit in.

CHAPTER 4

April 2011: Hawker And The Flinders Ranges

Last Fling With Civilisation

Wallowing in mall culture prior to heading for the Flinders Ranges and Nullarbor. Have a gourmet dinner and production catch-up with Leona, an old film crew member and friend - "Ah the good old shoot days where we had actual budgets and painkillers were for fun instead of anger management!" Her naughty puppy Ella is very cute.

James shows me his killer record collection and we end up with the kids and Honey all doing "stereo dancing" to Stanley Black and the Fred Silver Band (the Stilton of music cheese) while I make a stew. We stuff ourselves with second helpings while watching the poor wretch starve in his bus in "Into the Wild" and I uneasily try to laugh off the disturbing parallels to my Waggin' Trail adventure.

Note to self: Stock up on extra supplies of "Mighty Man" tinned meals.

James and I convince ourselves we both need to go to Ikea and have Swedish meatballs and manage to make it through with only one impulse-buy in the Market Hall. Then we go home and I help James put up an Expedit shelf using handy bits of wood from the shed. Amazingly, James assembles the shelf using only the required tool and parts.

Off to K.'s place tomorrow to plan the Flinders Ranges trip.

Camping Family Fun, or SHUT UP!!

Leave Adelaide with K., who has requested the nom de plume of "Old Fossil" (O.F.). First stop: Port Wakefield, which has nothing to recommend it so I won't mention it here. On to Port Augusta, where town planners thoughtfully greet arrivals with a scenic bridge over a water treatment pond called "Lake Knockout" (roll your windows up, that smell ain't the dog).

Arrive at beautiful Warren Gorge as dusk falls, discover Sooty hiding in the blankets, and a family with approximately twenty-seven toddlers arrives next to us. Three hours later they are still wrestling with the tent in the headlights of their car, providing us with much entertainment. The toddlers are sent into the bushes to collect firewood and snakebites. By midnight the family are ensconced in their tent and the crying and screaming begins.

"Guess there's bugger all chance of seeing any animals now," mutters the dad.

We go for a night walk and O.F. teaches me amazing constellation facts, which I am able to remember for about three minutes. There's probably an iphone app for it anyway. In the morning we go for a walk but it's clear from the number of trail bikes, children, football radio and generators that any yellow-footed rock wallabies are at least 3000 km away by now. So we hit the road, the fossils are calling.

Searching for Fossils

Driving quickly past many interesting historic and aboriginal art sites, we stop at Hawker to look at geological maps and enjoy lattés at the bakery with Horace and Doris, two small local dogs. O.F. mutters scientific incantations over her maps and stabs a finger at a tiny narrow formation called the Somethingambrian Layer. "We'll find

29

fossils here." We stock up on diesel ($5.62 a litre or thereabouts) and fridge magnets, then head northwest.

O.F. discovers a motherlode archeocyatha site at a location I have sworn to keep secret. We find some beauties! Archeocyatha were "sessile, reef-building marine organisms that lived during the early lower Cambrian period (approx. 500 million years ago)." In layperson's terms, ancient corals and squiddly diddly things. If you found one in your bathroom you would most likely spray it with Killex or smash it with a broom.

We make camp at Parachilna Gorge, which is certainly one of the top ten bush camping places in Australia - a stunning creek bed area lined with huge white-trunked gums and ancient red rock cliffs and hills. O.F. quickly makes a fire and I provide the evening's entertainment with a bottle of red and a good go on the didgeridoo. Honey begins to go feral. Sooty comes out and revels in the rustling bush noises of the night.

Gourmet Hot Rock Cooking

We spend the next day at our Parachilna site. A family of emus wanders through O.F.'s tent site and she fends off a stroppy teenage emu with her fossil hammer. I discover a thigh-deep water pool up the creek and have a refreshing dip. There's no one around and it's lovely to just wander up the shale-strewn hills and gullies, snooze in the sun and watch all the birds. O.F. is a dynamo and builds a hot rock oven in between fossil fossicking while I lie around reading about mad Amazonian explorers.

Dinner is a gourmet extravaganza of hot rock steaks, sweet corn, potatoes, apples, a light Clare Valley rosé and salad. Honey is now Camp Dog, lurking at the edge of the firelight and snatching any gnawed bones that the tribal elders fling into the darkness. We have pretty much stopped using cutlery.

From The Family Archives 1

It would be a pity at this point not to relate the oft-told tragi-comic story of a previous family venture into the Flinders Ranges several years ago. The trek involved my mum, her companion Peter, and my older brother Ben. They followed a similar route to mine and camped at Wilpena Pound in the popular tourist area.

It was high season and almost all the sites were occupied. Nonetheless, rules pertaining to quietness as night fell were followed to the dot. That is until mum and Peter - for some reason they have never been able to explain intelligently to the family – decided in the middle of the night that they wanted a couple of cookies (biscuits).

Under normal circumstances this would not be an alarming, disruptive impulse. However, here are the facts as reported by what turned out to be - in this instance – the delinquents:

- The cookies were in a bag in the car parked beside the tent.
- The car was a new model rental with an electronic alarm.
- Mum and Peter knew nothing about electronic car alarms.
- Ben, who knew how to use the electronic lock, was sound asleep in the tent, and Mum and Peter did not want to disturb him.
- Using a flashlight, they picked up the key-ring lying beside Ben's sleeping form, quietly unzipped the tent door and stepped out into the peace and stillness of the night, marvelling at the density of stars, with silhouettes of kangaroos grazing quietly nearby.
- They approached the car, (Mum and Peter – not the kangaroos) but knowing nothing about car alarms, then attempted to unlock it simply by using the door key.

- At which point all hell broke loose. – BEEEEP!! BEEEP!! BEEP!!
- They fumbled desperately with the unfamiliar gizmo on the key-ring, trying to keep their voices down. "Oh good God!!" "What have we done??" "How do we stop it?" " DO something for chrissakes!!" "We're going to get into TROUBLE!!"
- Lights began to go on inside other tents; Ben, now fully awake, said calmly through the tent wall, "Mum - just press the button on the back of the lock on the key-ring." Loud whispered response: "WHERE? WHAT BUTTON? Oh – found it." Then silence. Lights went out in tents. Calm was restored. Not a kangaroo or any other creature in sight – no doubt all had fled in terror.
- Desire for cookies had completely abated. They thought about having another go at opening one of the car doors but were now terrified at what the car – which they now believed had a mind of its own – might do next!
- Next morning, fearing the wrath of fellow campers, they cautiously unzipped the tent door, and poked their heads out, prepared to go around and apologize to everyone. In the event, there was no need. All the campsites had been vacated!

They say they still feel terrible about it. However, with the subsequent purchase of a new car, they have mastered the art of using electronic security keys.

CHAPTER 5

January 2012: Mesa

Bird's Eye View Of The Desert,
Or What Population Problem?

From thirty thousand feet the ground below us looks barren and uninhabited, like a picture of something sent back by the Mars Rovers or the more recent Curiosity remote explorer; a landscape veined with endless canyons and gullies, and then the biggest scar of all – the one visible from space – the Grand Canyon.

You marvel at the intrepid courage of early explorers like Colonel Wesley Powell who ventured into the maze of canyons relying for the most part on limited navigational skills, heading into unchartered territory that offered future opportunities or, more likely, certain death. No GPS recalculating for you in those days! Only the moon, stars, some survey skills and gut instinct. Little wonder that one cratered area out here was the training site for the early astronauts of the Apollo program. Only the vast distance from earth would have made the lunar landscape feel any more lonely and unfamiliar.

You find yourself wondering too about current claims that humans will overpopulate the planet to the point of self-destruction. Maybe the ones that adapt and survive will end up in places like this again, subsisting on minimal water and vegetation – repeating the history of earlier humans, perhaps reclaiming the old habitation sites of long-since devastated tribes like the aptly named Sinagua (without water) of Walnut Canyon near Flagstaff.

It's the kind of landscape that excites and terrifies at the same time – a push-pull kind of feeling. Semi desert; rocky outcrops that beckon from what seems a short distance in a broad landscape beneath a clear blue sky. But the deception can be lethal. Distances are much further than they appear. A two-hour hike suddenly turns into four, and without sufficient water a trip quickly shifts from fun to fatal.

From ground level the shapes and colours of the landscape: the red rock outcrops of cliffs and canyons contrasted with the sage green flora of grasses and cacti – bring back memories of trips in the Australian outback. Guide books in both countries warn of poisonous snakes and lizards, scorpions, and flash floods. They advise ceding a distance of at least ten feet to the creatures, and avoiding camping in dry river beds that can become raging torrents in a matter of seconds, sweeping away everything in their path.

Phoenix appears below us. The pilot tells us to prepare for landing. From the window we see several rocky mountain outcrops – many of them long-extinct volcanic cones - rising sharply from the desert floor. We're surprised at how close to the city some of them are. These are not massive ranges like the Rockies – nowhere near that kind of height. The outcrops reach heights of around 2,000 to 4,000 feet. Most have a distinctive name – Scarface, Usery Mountain, Camel Back, the Superstitions. All have history and legends attached to them – ancient sites long abandoned by their original inhabitants; goldmines purportedly found and then lost; die-hards who were sure they would rediscover them but ended up lost and died hard – usually of thirst. There'll be lots to explore and learn out here.

The aircraft taxis to a halt. We exit into the warm desert air.

"Have a good holiday," the young woman from the airport lounge calls to the old-timer.

"Sure will," he answers. "Gotta keep tryin' at my age!"

Don't we all? I think to myself......*Don't we all?*

Arrival

Nothing can quite match the unspeakable bliss of flying into instant summer! We take off a couple of long-sleeved layers and head for the baggage claim. It feels good here already.

We are surprised at the friendliness of the people as we make our way to the car rental shuttle. I don't quite know what we expected. Americans get such negative press a lot of the time, yet in our travels we have almost always found them to be open and amiable. Maybe online reviews of airports and services are only written by grumpy people! The sites we had scrutinized on the internet seemed to complain of difficulties finding specific areas in Phoenix Sky Harbour airport, with minimal or non-existent help from staff. Maybe they hadn't learned to read or something. There are clear signs posted everywhere. Helpful airport volunteers approach if they think you look lost or confused. Their common question seems to be, "Have you come from Canada?" It is only much later in our stay that we will come to realize the significance of this.

We find the car rental shuttle bus pretty easily. It's very well-organized. A ten minute drive on the shuttle bus brings us to the central car rental location, the reservation is in order and we are soon in our small car and on our way. As we pass the exit booth, the attendant asks, "How was our service today?" We tell him "Fantastic." He grins. He's pleased.

We head for the major highway to battle our way to the wilds of Mesa. The GPS is plugged into the cigarette lighter socket and springs to life, the familiar robot voice instructing us "In 400 meters keep right onto ramp." We follow it slavishly as we try to come to terms with five lanes of traffic on each side of the highway, such a shock in contrast to sleepy old White Rock we have left far behind. After a half hour of stress, we are told, "Arriving at Sunset Acres, on right," and there we see the welcoming flags and entrance gate. We have made it. Here we go.......

Tryin' out a Trailer

When you Google-Earth Mesa, the camera swooshes down, flying over what looks like one vast, never-ending trailer park. You wonder if anyone there lives in an actual "real" house. There seem to be major roads everywhere – we think the noise must be awful. But here we are. We pull up to the security kiosk by the automatic gates, and a friendly (of course!) attendant welcomes us. We are expected. The gates are opened up to let us in.

Several things strike us right away. Firstly, there is no noise from the main avenue we have just left behind. Secondly, the place seems to be laid out like a small village with tidy, narrow roadways. Thirdly, the people we pass on our way to the central administration building all smile and wave. Fourthly, everywhere is clean, tidy and quiet. The rows of little Park Model mobile homes are all well-kept, with desert-style landscaping – rocks and cacti, palm trees, citrus trees abundant with oranges and grapefruit. Each little dwelling announces its number and ownership with a small plaque out front.

We worry that it's possibly what a Thomas Kincaid version of a trailer park might be or even the scary "perfect" town in *The Truman Show* from which you can never escape because the roads lead to nowhere.

Or worse still, we wonder if, at the end of our month's stay we shall find ourselves screaming, "I am not a number!" as we are hauled off in straitjackets like Patrick McGoohan in the quaint-looking village in *The Prisoner*. It makes us nervous.

Settling In

We park outside the main administration and recreation centre and go to the Business Office. We need to find Hank who has the keys to the unit we are renting. We've arrived earlier than expected and are told Hank is in the kitchen cooking for a big social event scheduled for this evening. Through the swing doors to the ballroom and social events area we follow our noses to the source of the delicious smells drifting through more swinging doors at the far end of the huge room – and here it is - the kitchen.

It's a hub of activity. Huge pots on restaurant-size stove tops; people stirring, slicing, chopping, tasting; and hovering over a steaming pot is the guy we've checked on the photograph we were given – Hank. Grey-haired, with grey beard and glasses, wrapped in a chef's apron, he's totally focused on his culinary task, but when we tentatively call his name he looks up right away, smiles and says, "Ha! You're early! Just hang on a minute, this is almost ready." Canadian-style we apologise for interrupting his food preparation, "Sorry."

He removes the apron from his portly middle and accompanies us to the Business Office where he checks us in and introduces us to the staff and we pay a small fee for the phone, cable and internet connection. Hank then walks us over to one of the little Park Model houses – the one we are renting for a month. He hands us the keys, shows us around and explains how things work, and then has to hurry back to his cooking.

"Anything you need or want to know, just call me any time," he calls with a cheerful wave. We go back inside and explore our new living space, relaxing our faces from the aches of the fixed Miss America smiles we now realize we have been flashing around so as to look as friendly as everyone else.

The efficient use of space in the little trailer home is amazing. Nothing is wasted – a corner cupboard here, a fold-out laundry hamper there. More cupboard and drawer space than you would ever imagine in such a small place. We find ourselves wondering how humans ever became obsessed with huge, immovable houses – weren't we all once nomads? Here one day, off to somewhere new tomorrow, carrying our house-building materials along with us or starting over fresh?

Suddenly, our 1800 square foot home back in Canada starts to seem unnecessarily extravagant, with some rooms we barely even use or venture into anymore, now that we're empty-nesters and have sold our basement-operated business. What are we filling the rooms with? Stuff we think we need but can actually do without when our space is much more limited.

There's "stuff" in the trailer too of course. Something in the human psyche seems to need to fill empty spaces, be they on floors or walls. I wonder why? Do the unnecessary possessions reassure us that we are alive, that we exist, that we have "taste" in whatever shape or form it takes?

Back home for a long time we displayed souvenir collections from our numerous travels, but now with our increasingly advancing ages we've started giving things away to make room for the more recent memorabilia. Maybe this is why people move into bigger houses – to accommodate the accumulations of travels, photo albums, changes in taste.

Recently we did a "blitz" and seem to have reduced the museum pieces to an Australian didgeridoo and a replica set of small terracotta clay warrior pieces purchased from a souvenir stand for all of $1.50 in Xian – home of the tomb of the mad Chinese emperor Qin.

The trailer home is no exception to the space-filling syndrome. People here seem to feel that a certain amount of "clutter" gives places a homey feeling. Maybe for them it does. The unit we have rented leaves no blank wall area undecorated.

So we have small wire-made ukuleles, plaster and plastic ornaments of Mexican and native people doing "traditional" things like smoking peace pipes, or sitting out front with their arms round their knees, sombreros covering their faces having a siesta – the racist "lazy latino" stereotype (do people never learn??); strings of plastic fruit hanging on the wall that you keep bashing into when you walk past; china plates with Significant Things written on them, strategically placed on shelves so high up that you can't read The Message; native dream-catchers; baskets of dried and artificial flowers that shed their bits every time you walk past; a "cute" doll on a high shelf over the TV, in traditional native polyester dress; two big red plastic butterflies climbing up the wall in the bathroom, and of course abundant photos of the happy owners and their family – the memories and souvenirs that somehow validate people's lives, reassuring them of their existence.

We all do it in one way or another. Even in the pharaonic tombs of Ancient Egypt we had been amazed to see ancient Roman graffiti scrawled on the walls, announcing to archaeologists and tourists alike that "Marcus" or whomever "was here." In Latin of course.

Much later we also discover that having lots of ornaments and stuff on walls seems very important in trailer living, for on being shown what we thought was quite a restrained unit that was for sale, the agent commented, "Typical bachelor place, right? Very basic. No ornaments or anything. Doesn't show well at all". (We didn't choose it – not because of the lack of ornaments but because the unit was too close to the garbage bin collection area. But this was all in the future.)

For now, we are fascinated with the place we are renting but wonder how long we can survive the demands of a much reduced living space. Will we be going mad by the end of the month, sitting on the porch sharpening knives and slyly eyeing each other speculatively through half-closed eyes?

Once we have got our minimal stuff unpacked and put away, we forage for food at a local supermarket, and then set about exploring what the resort has to offer.

Quite a lot as it turns out, though not all of what's available will be to our choosing. We decide to skip the woodworking and quilting classes; but we reserve one of the courts for a game of tennis, and I sign up for Zumba. I also see a notice about the tennis All Play, which takes place Monday through Friday from 4 p.m. to 5:30 p.m. I ask someone what it means, and it sounds like fun. I decide it's worth checking out later – I'm still a bit overwhelmed and anxious as to what is expected of us. I wonder if it's competitive or what?

On the Activities bulletin board we find information about hiking in local regional and state parks which are a mere 15 – 30 minute drive away. The two swimming pools and Jacuzzis are ours to use whenever we wish. I see a sign-up list for line dancing, which I've always wanted to try, but it clashes with Zumba. We're going to be busy!

CHAPTER 6

April 2011: Flinders Ranges and Port Germein

A Mistaken Assumption

We pack up and I beep Sooty's locator; we can hear it clearly in the bus so I assume that she is in her usual hidey hole. We stop in Blinman (pop. 7) and have breakfast at the general store. Excellent selection of fridge magnets. Refreshed after a terrifying thirty-six hours without lattés, we make our way towards Wilpena Pound, pausing to look at the Great Wall of China rock formation.

Wilpena Pound was the site of yet another episode in the earlier ill-fated expedition undertaken by the trio of family members. Here are the details:

From The Family Archives 2

With calm and sanity reasonably restored at the campsite, Mum, Peter and Ben resumed their hiking around Wilpena Pound and took a flight like the one I plan to do tomorrow with O.F.

Then two days after the calamitous incident with the car, Mum got up early to walk down the narrow access road to the washrooms. It was a clear day, the sun was just clearing the surrounding hills and casting its morning rays on the mountains - your archetypical Aussie wilderness awe-inspiring scene. Entranced by the spectacle of the sunrise on the cliffs, Mum unexpectedly stepped into a deep pothole in the dirt track. She said she heard a kind of snap, and at first assumed she had trodden on twigs or debris in the hole as she fell to the ground.

41

The sharp pain in her left ankle told her all was not well. The ankle began to swell, she could barely stand, and became nauseous. Nobody was around, so she staggered back to the tent where Ben – who is a walking emergency clinic – pulled out ice packs and pain killers. By now the ankle was an interesting shade of purple and Mum a shade of green. After administering first aid and making her comfortable, Ben and Peter knew they had to get her to a hospital for x-ray. But where??

Hawker was the nearest town with a hospital, so they drove there and helped Mum limp into the emergency entrance. Details were taken by the nurses on duty, but an x-ray would not be possible until the doctor (the flying variety, this being a remote part of Australia) showed up, which could be several hours as he was in the air en route to a cattle station further up north.

The nurses took a look at the ankle, said that it did indeed look nasty, but that since Mum had managed to limp in, it could possibly be just a bad sprain. Grasping at anything that would avoid wasting valuable holiday time sitting around for hours, Mum went along with this possibility. The nurses wrapped a support bandage around the ankle, handed Mum a bottle of Tylenol and waved goodbye as the trio drove off back to Wilpena Pound in time to take the spectacular flight over the ranges.

Mum continued to limp around for the remaining two weeks of the holiday, being careful how she placed her foot down with each step, taking as much weight as possible on her walking poles. The pain gradually subsided, but she kept the tensor bandage on for good measure, and was wearing it when she visited her doctor back in Canada.

The doctor removed the bandage, examined the ankle (which was no longer swollen), pressed and felt around the bones and ordered an immediate x-ray. It was a case of good news and bad news, and the doctor was less than pleased with what she described as reckless stupidity.

"That was really silly, walking around in Australian wilderness on a broken ankle," she said. "Do you realize how lucky you've been? Fortunately it has healed in-line, otherwise I would have had to break and reset it!" Mum felt quite faint at the thought and got a sudden flash image of Kathy Bates in *Misery*, just before she breaks both of James Caan's ankles in order to render him immobile.

Sooty Goes AWOL

Today Wilpena Pound is full of tourists as usual; O.F. and I take a short walk, encounter a pair of emus, then head to Rawnsley Park Station which is a big multipurpose tourist campground. It turns out to be dog friendly and although it's busy we're given a fantastic hilltop campsite. Nestled in a valley on the southwestern edge of the Pound, our campground provides stunning views but more importantly they have a SWIMMING POOL. I'm in. It's heaven. We also book ourselves a scenic flight for next morning.

Back at the bus, there's still no sign of Sooty. I'm worried, and we hope that she's just out exploring and will do her usual thing of sneaking into my bed at three in the morning. Trying to keep cheerful, I set up a "stage" on our camping table for O.F. who puts on her belly dancing gear and we fire up Ivan Rebroff on the record player and take photos of her doing her shimmy thing, surrounded by solar fairy lights.

View From The Air

Crack of dawn, I emerge from Waggin' Trail to see a huge orange hot air balloon drifting past, wake up O.F. to have a look. No sign of Sooty and I am really perplexed. She is impossible to find during daylight, so I agree to go ahead with our scenic flight and then work out a search plan.

The flight is stunning! O.F.'s knowledge of the area is amazing and she takes over the tour commentary. Our pilot, who is about 17 years old, lets me briefly fly the plane. I turn down the volume on my headset as O.F.'s screams become distracting. As we make a very steep banking turn we see how huge and complex the Pound is, and fly over Waggin' Trail!

On landing I leave O.F. to the horrors of the caravan park and set off for Parachilna to start searching for little Sooty. I spend most of the night driving and walking at all our stopping points, beeping her locator and calling and waiting, but no luck.

The next morning I make up a bunch of flyers and start posting them along the roadsides and in Blinman, stopping and searching each time. Everyone in Blinman is very kind and helpful. One woman thinks she might have seen Sooty near the shop, and suggests I contact her son down at Wilpena to see if he would be able to look for her during the week. I head down to Wilpena; he can't do it, but one of the guys lends me a cat trap and I head back to the caravan park.

Back at the caravan park I discover that O.F. has become a star attraction with the campers following her contributions to the fossil lecture and she is even giving didgeridoo lessons. I also find out she has been reading a Mills and Boon romance novel from the laundry and: WATCHING TELEVISION. The abandonment of her lifelong bush lore is evident in an incomplete hot rock firepit project next to her tent. We get dressed up and go out for dinner at the Woolshed, which compares unfavorably to our fire pit cooking and we have trouble readjusting to using knives and forks.

After dinner, I head back to resume my night watch for Sooty in Blinman. Up most of the night, no luck. Everyone is on the lookout and the locals have put the flyers up around town. There doesn't seem to be much else I can do, so I finally head back to the caravan park. After so much long driving and little sleep I am dispirited and exhausted. O.F. is very kind and reassuring.

Sooty Where Are You?

Right now feeling sad as I have lost little Sooty in the Flinders Ranges. I thought both cats were happily ensconced at my friend K.'s place in Adelaide, only to discover Sooty had stowed away in the bedding in Waggin' Trail when we got to the ranges.

All was fine during the trip until one morning I beeped her locator collar and heard it go off in the bus, and so I headed off with O.F. assuming Sooty was on board. What I didn't know was that there was a gap in the battery housing under the bus and she was actually in there and not in the bus itself. So when we got to our next campsite at the end of the day, no Sooty - she'd hopped out somewhere en route. I still think she is probably in Blinman; everyone in the town is keeping their eye out for her.

I have hardly slept and feel terrible that I didn't know about the battery housing thing. The best I can hope for is that she will turn up at someone's house and they will phone her in (she's got tags, microchip etc). At least she is a good hunter and will probably survive OK. She has always been very independent, but I feel so worried for her and angry at myself for not checking more carefully. Fingers crossed.

Port Germein

Strange humid weather, rain coming. Port Germein is an odd little place with the best junk shop you have ever seen. It seems noteworthy for having built what appears to be the longest wooden jetty in the southern hemisphere, on massive tidal flats, and then not using it for anything. The water is crystal clear.

Here for two nights then on to Port Augusta so that Waggin' Trail can have a good pre-flight check prior to the Nullarbor.

Once again asking for an unpowered site gets me a primo spot in the tiny, cramped caravan park. Despite being metres from the sweeping water views of Yorke Peninsula and the Southern Flinders Ranges, it is designed so that any scenic views are carefully obscured by corrugated amenity buildings and eye-level fences.

CHAPTER 7

January 2012: Call Of The Desert

The Rules.

There are rules. We don't mind rules; it's one of the reasons we moved into a gated condo community back home. Living, even in higher-end suburbs seems to have its hazards nowadays – guys doing car maintenance and oil changes in their driveways; parents who go away for a weekend leaving teenagers unsupervised and hence the inevitable party-swarming leading to property damage, a police stand-off, and the usual denial on the part of the hastily-recalled parents....."She'd *never* do such a thing!" And the teenage perpetrators with their Jekyll-and-Hyde personalities standing there, the smirks and aggression evident in their faces a few moments ago now transformed into trembling-lip expressions of victimhood, claims of police abuse and total innocence.

So yes, there are rules at the trailer park and we like 'em; and they are *real* rules, not the "suggestions" that many rules and laws seem to pass for these days. These rules are *enforced*. Otherwise what's the point of having any?

Of course, coming from benign, apologetic Canada ("Sorry!") some rules are a bit startling because this is America and we haven't yet absorbed the ethos of the American mind-set – especially where firearms are involved. So the gun rule is a bit alarming – we're not used to seeing warnings about personal gun use or ownership in campsites and resorts! But here it is, loud and clear :

> *"Public display of firearms is prohibited unless you are a city, county, state or federal law enforcement officer and required to always have immediate access to a weapon."*

We're not sure if this adds to, or detracts from, our sense of safety and security! Our experienced neighbours from back home tell us that just about every American resident in the resort "packs heat". One woman who regularly goes for a healthy walk, apparently always takes a small hand gun along with her, stowed in her fanny-pack – just in case, I suppose. We decide to play ostrich and metaphorically bury our heads in the desert sand – we just don't want to know.

I wonder if gun owners are allowed in the structured Thomas Kincaid or Disney villages? Probably, since the right to bear arms is so deeply entrenched in the American psyche. It all seems a bit incongruous and puzzling, as though they are not so much afraid of foreign invasion, as they are of each other – a point well illustrated by Michael Moore in his documentary *Bowling for Columbine.*

In the documentary, Moore goes to Toronto, Canada, to check out if what he has heard about people not locking their doors is true. He finds that it is. Opening people's unbolted front doors on a busy street, he is greeted by owners inside who ask if he is lost or needs help. He asks one woman if she is afraid, and she replies with a smile, "No. Should I be?"

He bids goodbye to one owner saying, "Thanks for not shooting me."

Anyway, the rules here are mostly just sensible, reasonable demands geared to ensuring that everyone has a pleasant time in pleasant surroundings. There won't be any oil changes going on here, that's for sure, and we're happy with that.

Quiet time is officially mandated from 11 p.m. to 7:30 a.m. but we soon notice after moving in that there is neither sight nor sound of anyone or anything after around 8 p.m. The odd light shines from some units, but most of the resort population seems to be sound asleep by then.

After several days of activities that start around 9 a.m. for us, and that include a morning run or dance class, followed by a two-hour hike, lunch, tennis, swimming and finally a spell in one of the Jacuzzis, we're as ready to hit the sack as everyone else!

First Days In A Trailer

We find that the peace and tranquility of the resort are deceptive – nicely so – for upon exiting into the outside world we discover we are within close and easy access to several shopping areas for our food foraging and banking needs. A very convenient feature of the large supermarkets here is that they also have a small but full-on version of one of the major banks incorporated into their stores. It's just one of the many features you come across that make life that little bit easier, and we like it.

The next thing we notice is that in general, food here is much cheaper – except for the specialist vegetarian brands we like; but that's the same back home too. What looks to us like a good $150 worth of sustenance in our shopping cart, comes to less than $100. And wherever we go, and whatever we shop for, we are almost always offered a discount deal. It's almost as if it is considered a crime to charge or pay full price for anything! Sometimes there's an additional discount for being a senior. Even in restaurants we are guided through various wheelings and dealings to get the best low price................

Sample encounter:

Us: "We'd like the pasta with a side salad, please."

Server: "That's great. But if you add one more side, it counts as the Thursday Special and you get 20% off – and you're seniors, right? So you get a free dessert as well. Okay?"

At this rate, you start thinking that with a bit of effort you could get them to pay YOU for eating there!

We drive back with our groceries, get everything efficiently put away, and then sit down and figure out what we want to do tomorrow. The weather is fabulous – pleasantly warm. We decide to check out the nearest desert recreation area – Usery Mountain Regional Park.

Call Of The Desert

A fifteen minute drive brings us to the park entrance and we pull into the parking lot by the Nature Centre. The desert hiking is the big pull for us so we pick up brochures and trail maps at the Nature Centre. Although the park is close to the edge of the city, once you get onto the trails and into the hills,  you quickly leave civilization behind. You're in a land of sand and cacti: saguaro, prickly pear, jumping cholla, hedgehog cacti, palo verde trees, ocotillo, mesquite and creosote shrubs. That's the flora.

In the fauna category there are snakes (rattlers), desert fox, tortoises, lizards, gila monsters (the only poisonous lizards in North America) and birds galore. From time to time there are the familiar warnings of flash floods in the washes. It's easy to see how some people get caught on a warm sunny day with not a cloud in sight.

Since this first visit is supposed to be a scouting survey, we don't intend to do any full-on trail work; we have only brought one bottle of water and an orange between us and an energy snack each – no proper lunch or anything. We're immediately intrigued with what one of the rangers at the Centre tells us about the most popular trail that goes up to a cave. We decide just to scout out the trailhead for future serious hiking.

The parking area at the trailhead is quickly found. We jump out of the car and look up at the striated, sand-coloured mountain cliff face before us. Maybe we should just check out the first stretch of the trail and see what it's like under foot.

We set off, and then become brain-dead. All our common sense disappears, and we find ourselves saying, "Just up to that next rise," ……."Just round that next bend," …..and "It can't be that far away now."

The sun is high in the sky now and the cool morning breeze is no more. We're starting to wilt. A ranger comes towards us heading back down the trail.

"Are we nearly there yet?" we ask her, like a couple of pre-schoolers on a tedious school outing.

"You're not too far away," she answers, leaving us to wonder what her scale of reference is for terms like "far" and "near".

"About fifteen to twenty minutes, and there's some scrambling at the point where the trail gets quite narrow."

She strides off, confident in her youthful ability to make her legs and feet do what she demands of them ……not like some of us.

We decide not to risk it today. We've already been going for over an hour. There's hardly any water left and we only have the orange to share between us. We've already overstretched our resources. So we turn and head down. We'll tackle this one again another day when we're properly prepared. Descents at our age are sometimes more challenging than ascents; knees don't behave the way you want them to anymore; sometimes they feel as if they are going to bend backwards! It's worse if, like me, you've undergone past surgeries on one of them.

So the descent involves a fair amount of whining on my part. I'm hot, thirsty, didn't bring my poles for support, and want to blame Peter for everything:

"Why didn't you : remind me to bring my poles? / make us turn around sooner? / bring more water?" etc. etc.

But he's not a psychologist for nothing; he stays calm and encouraging and hands me all the remaining water to drink. In my increasingly dark frame of mind I think to myself, *"He's such a good person – he'll go to heaven when he dies, and he'll only have himself to blame!"* Not nice.

Then the trail flattens out and we can see the parking lot a few hundred yards ahead. Refuge! I gulp down the last drops of water and stagger to the drinking fountain outside the washroom building, feeling like an extra in one of the old black and white desert war movies - *Ice Cold in Alex* comes to mind, where John Mills & co. stagger into a bar in Alexandria after days crossing the desert, and order ice cold beer with a good froth on top. Sooo good.

In the car we turn on the air conditioning and drive on to check other trail heads we see on the map. Before leaving the park we check at the Nature Centre one more time, and pick up a list of scheduled events. It's a smorgasbord of delights. We tick off the activities we'd like to do: ranger-guided bird spotting; identifying animal tracks and dens; and we sign up for   lectures on the

Ancient Peoples of the Desert, and The Geology of Arizona. Then we return to the resort, realizing it is going to seem like a very short month's visit living in the trailer.

CHAPTER 8

May 2011: Port Augusta – Fowlers Bay

Mouse Attack And Cat-Tales

So this morning I open the cupboard and someone - someone SMALL and MOUSE SIZED - has nibbled a perfect hole in the Hungarian paprika bag, then rolled wildly in it all over the bottom of the cupboard. I'm talking about a pretty big bag of paprika too, it's not like it nibbled into the bag and then went, "Oh, whoops." No. This mouse cut into the bag with the precision of a high tech diamond thief, then texted its friends "U R INV8D 2 PAPRIKA ORGY LOL" and went berserk in a kind of spice wallowing frenzy.

This means that somewhere in the bus is at least one bright orange mouse. I have spoken with Smokey about this as it falls to his department to rectify any mouse type situations, but as he pointed out he prefers his mice "al dente, with a sprinkling of basil" and paprika is not in his contract.

I leave Port Germein and Port Augusta behind and head for Wudinna which lays claim to the second largest monolith in Australia (and no – Ayers Rock is NOT the biggest one; Mount Augustus is twice as big and a long way from where we are right now).

Made of granite, Mount Wudinna lies some 12 kms outside the town. It's an impressive site rising some 260 metres (about 865 feet) above the plain. Smokey the intrepid feline companion decides an expedition is warranted. Here is an extract from his log:

A TAIL IN THE WILDERNESS

> *Expedition Goal:*
> *Mt. Wudinna*
> *Summit, previously*
> *unclimbed by cats.*

Let no cat say that he has not the heart of a lion, nor the soul of a god; to conquer fear and surpass all misgivings, to rise above any limits, hold high his head and say, "I am lord of all I survey, a king among all creatures, and though I tread alone, my conquering footsteps lead where all cats may follow."

The ascent in
progress

The summit
achieved.

Playing With Dolphins And Sea Lions

AWESOME. Today is why I set off on the Waggin' Trail adventure. Alan, a local tour guide and boatman takes a small group of us campers out to swim with dolphins and sea lions off Jones Island. As the dolphins charge towards you and start playing you don't care about how cold the water is. The water is quite shallow, just a couple of metres, and the dolphins are close enough to touch, rolling over and swimming upside down - if you do the same, they come back and do it again.

The dolphins follow us half a km over to the island itself, surfing the bow wave of the boat. The sea lions rush over and soon they're all playing chasey and checking us out. I can't get into the water fast enough; it's crystal clear and the sea lions and dolphins are all around us.

I'm blown away when one of the younger sealions comes up and gives me a gentle nuzzle on my face mask! It loves having its chin scratched and bumps against me for more nuzzling, just like a big friendly dog. It grabs a bit of seaweed and teases me, wanting to play "catch me". I swear it's laughing. At one point there's a crazy tangle of us - humans and sea lions - all nuzzling, patting and just being silly.

The dolphins race back into the mob and the sea lions chase them a few metres away to the surf, where they all start surf-racing each other and leaping out of the water, coming back occasionally to try and get us clumsy humans to join in. But we're all exhausted; back in the boat for a mug of hot chocolate, then reluctantly heading back to shore.

Smokey's waiting for me on the beach and we walk back to the campsite together, and I think, this is what is possible between animals and humans when we share instead of control, when we can just be together and notice the ways in which we're all the same. Not sure if it would work with sharks though – nuzzling noses and scratching under chins (do sharks have chins??)......maybe not. There are limits if both parties don't understand or abide by the rules! But still ....

Ticking off the Sights

A kind of "tick the box" sightseeing day along the coast towards Streaky Bay. Inselbergs called "Murphy's Haystacks" fall into the "WEIRD OR WHAT?" category, then long boring drive along more desolate coastal plains to Westall Way, which is dramatic but mostly just views rather than places to walk.

Pause in Streaky Bay to fill up with water and buy insanely expensive groceries, then onward to another tiny fishing village called Haslam where the campground is PACKED with grey nomads relaxing next to their rows of generators. In keeping with traditional Aussie caravan park design, the site is placed on the beachfront in such a way that the only view is of a large abandoned shed and some rubbish bins. Smokey alights from the bus and rapidly becomes a sensation with fans gathering around.

From the jetty, as the sun sets, I can see the hazy flat coastline of the Nullarbor disappearing off into forever. There will be no more shopping malls for at least 1300 kilometres. How will we survive?

Fowler's Bay

I check out some of the scenic side roads as we approach Fowler's Bay - the famous Cactus Beach surf hangout, Point Sinclair. Corrugated roads jar all my fillings loose and Smokey clings to the corners of the desk top with a "this is most undignified" look on his face. After 10 km of bone rattling and the bus sounding like it's coming to pieces I have second thoughts about my ambitious plans of doing the Gibb River Road.

We arrive at Fowler's Bay (pop. 3) where we are again greeted by the obligatory corrugated scenic view at the beachfront caravan park. But the people are nice and we meet Fowler the cat. Smokey and Honey come for a long walk up the massive sand dunes behind the town; both of them go nuts and run around madly, and we all run crazily down the side of a huge dune.

Honey and Smokey are a big hit at the communal campfire. Everyone is very friendly and jokey, it's nice to have a social evening for a change. I learn how you can collect rainwater using a collapsible bucket, and how to catch squid. It's also interesting to hear the reasons why others are travelling and living on the road. There are older single people who have lost partners and are travelling as a way of recovering, others who, like me, just got fed up with running businesses and paying crazy bills. One couple is travelling with an older autistic son; others with a partner who is terminally ill.

My age group seems to be rare, and the older roadsters are very kind and supportive. It is disturbing when I am the one to bring up 12 volt power systems as an interesting topic of campfire chat, and before you know it, I and another lady are deep in conversation about caravan towing courses and power system options for portable washing machines.

Sooty Sighting?

The lovely lady at Blinman Mine Tours (north of Wilpena Pound) reckons she has spotted Sooty! So she is now putting out food and calling her and will let me know if she manages to catch her. The description of the cat she saw sounds very much like Sooty, so fingers crossed!

CHAPTER 9

January 2012: The Call Of The Not-So-Faraway Hills
(With apologies to whoever wrote the theme music for *Shane*)

Desert Hiking

Having come from sea level back home in Canada, up to this higher country, we start off doing the less strenuous trails. Need to break ourselves in gradually. So we do a couple of fairly gentle loops first, two or three-hour round-trip hikes. It's cool when we hit the trails in the morning, and we wear at least three layers; but it's not long before we start removing them once we get moving and the sun gets higher in the sky.

Side trails take us up over a rise, and from the top we see the huge desert valley floor spread below us, stretching way out into the blue haze of distant mountain ranges whose names we shall need to look up later. In between, numerous volcanic cones rise so symmetrically they could be mistaken for artificial mounds perhaps left over from the numerous silver and copper mining enterprises during the late 1800's and into the 1900s; however, the cinder cones are the residue of perfectly natural phenomena in a zone that was subjected to frequent volcanic activity millions of years ago.

These are my favourite vistas – the kind of limitless expanses as far as you can see. It's easy to understand why people who lived centuries ago believed the world was flat and that if they walked far enough they'd disappear over the edge, never to be seen or heard from again.

It's an entirely different experience from the hiking we have access to back home in British Columbia. There, you embark on a mountain trail winding through forests of massive fir, pine and cedar trees – impressive enough in their own beautiful way. The trail winds upwards in switchback fashion, with rarely a glimpse of what lies below and beyond, so that (in our case) we sometimes start thinking maybe we've missed a turn or something, because didn't we just do this stretch already?

To be sure, there's usually the reward of a spectacular view once the summit is reached, but for me the process is less appealing than being able to stop at any time and feast my eyes on a landscape that at least allows you to physically see and judge how far you have travelled for your efforts.

Close Encounters With Cacti

We follow a trail that loops around the lower levels of the park, trying to recall the names of the different cacti from hikes we've done in the past. The prickly pear cactus is etched in my memory from a nasty encounter with one many years ago………

I was bent over taking a close-up shot of a prickly pear in bloom and inadvertently (stupidly) stepped backwards into a large one right behind me. I was wearing shorts, and being bent over left a portion of my upper leg and rear end exposed. It felt as though something had attacked me with dozens of red-hot sewing needles!

A good half hour was spent with Peter carefully extracting the large number of cactus spines one by one while I lay face down on the back seat of the car, moaning and trying to see it as a sure-fire learning experience.

It's true that you can have all kinds of knowledge in your head, but it's of no practical use to you until something actually happens. As Laurie Faria Stolartz is reputed to have said: "You need to screw up to learn." Yes indeed. The only caveat I would add in these times of what

I call *synthetic experience*, is that the experience needs to be *real* as opposed to *virtual*. You can't replicate surviving a mountaineering mishap by twiddling away on a high-tek tablet or smart phone. It has to really happen to you. Real experiences now seem to have been so mediated by movies and video games that people tend to believe they have been through the real events depicted in them. There are even movie stars who have succombed to this delusion, especially where World War II films are concerned!

Anyway, since the prickly pear episode I haven't made that particular mistake. And I treat all cacti with respect and give them distance – even the grasses out here have tiny self-protecting spines that will penetrate the toughest gardening gloves you can find at Home Depot.

The tall saguaros are unmistakable. At one point we  can see, about half a kilometre away, a splendid archetypal saguaro absolutely perfect in shape, its central stem reaching skyward for what must surely be a good twenty feet, maybe more, its branches stretched out like the arms of a supplicant on either side. We decide to check it out on our way back. This one's too good to miss.

We continue on, noting Teddy Bear or Jumping Cholla forests, stands of ocotillo, the ubiquitous Prickly Pear and Barrel-Fishhook cacti, patches of Hedgehog cacti, and Palo Verde trees everywhere, many of them already invaded by clusters of parasitic mistletoe which we had at first thought to be birds' nests. The mistletoe is destructive to the trees of course, but provides food for birds in the form of its sticky berries. Nature's version of win-some-lose-some and co-operative living.

We drop down into a shallow wash, come up the other side, turn down a bend in the trail and after another kilometre voilà, there is our perfect saguaro right ahead of us. Except – surprise! surprise! - It isn't a saguaro at all. It's the microwave transmitting and receiving tower for the park in clever, creative disguise! The ultimate in camouflage.

Over a series of days we cover a goodly number of the trails, including the one to the cave which, unbelievably, we discover we can see from the kitchen window of the trailer! This time, when we take it on, we are prepared with plenty of water and snacks. Turns out we were indeed not very far from the top of the mountainside on our first abortive attempt.

The so-called cave itself is a bit of a disappointment. It's hardly what you imagine a cave to be. No hole-in-the wall with a clearly-defined entrance into dark nether regions. It's just a hollow eroded out by the elements, with a wide packed-mud platform and low rock wall, that looks out across the valley to the northwest; the sort of strategic spot earlier peoples most likely used as a safe dwelling area. Worth the climb though.

On a couple of evenings we drive out to the nature centre for the lectures. We are surprised at the number of people who attend the lectures on geology and ancient peoples of the region. The lecture room at the nature centre is packed and more chairs have to be brought out from storage. Ages range from small babies through to old folks like ourselves. Everyone listens attentively and there are plenty of questions.

They are fascinating topics, made more so by the fact that we have all been interacting with the very environments that are being described and shown on the PowerPoint display. There are lessons too – plenty to think about as the speakers quietly point out the implications for our future as humans in this area. Some of the catastrophic events seem destined for a repeat performance – lack of water followed by desolation being one possible scenario. Lots of good disaster movie material here.

Myths, Legends And Superstitions

Before our time in Arizona is up, we head out to the Superstition Mountains. We do one pretty straightforward hiking loop. The feel of this area seems quite different than the desert hiking we have done over the past few days and weeks in the area closer to the trailer park. Perhaps it is the name that lends a bit of a sinister atmosphere; and the mountains that seem to loom over us in a threatening way – or could it be that the recent crash of a small aircraft, killing all on board, is shaping our reactions to the sheer, ominously vertical cliffs? Rescuers had a very difficult time reaching the wreckage; the jagged outcrops did not render up their victims willingly. Yet once again, it is incredible that this was all well within sight of the valley cities.

The history of this part of the desert seems to be comprised of many legends that have intrigued and confounded hikers and explorers since the late 19th. century. It has one of the most famous and pervasive "lost gold" legends, enhanced by the commonly reputed "curse", like the tomb of some Egyptian pharaohs.

More than 8000 people are reputed to have searched for the gold, many suffering strange deaths or disappearances. There are tales of lost goldmines and the mysterious deaths of those who later tried to locate them. Tales of headless bodies discovered in the Superstition wilderness, of secrets told and explorations thwarted; of phantom sniper protectors killing anyone coming close to finding the legendary goldmine, and even as recently as 2010 the disappearance of three hikers whose bodies were only discovered a year later. Official autopsy attributed the deaths to dehydration.

Added to all this ghostly-ghastly history of legend is the intriguing fact that at least one geologist has pointed out that no gold could possibly be found in the Superstitions since they are made of igneous rock! But like alien abductions, the number of willing believers shows no sign of dwindling anytime soon.

The one loop we circumnavigate gives enough of a sense of the wilderness out there, but further excursions will have to wait for now. We return to the trailer park feeling a bit spooked.

CHAPTER 10

May 2011: The Nullarbor

A Little Bit Of Latin

So - all those who have studied Latin please raise your hands........I thought so. Well, since you're all dying to know – Nullarbor is two Latin words : *Null* (meaning *None*) and *arbor* (meaning *tree*) – get it? So it's a vast barren, treeless area that lies parallel to the Great Australian Bight. The

Eyre Highway skirts the southern edge of the Nullarbor Plain. It connects Port Augusta in South Australia and Norseman in Western Australia. It's a v e r y l o o oo n g waaay .... almost 1670 kms long; one section of it runs for 146 kms with no curves or bends. It is claimed (by some internet sources) to be the longest straight stretch of road in the world. So here we go.......

Sooty Postscript:
The Price Of Freedom Is Freedom

Before we head out, I take a few moments of silence to reflect on the loss of our beloved feline companion, little Sooty. Smokey and Honey seem to pick up on my mood and wait patiently at their travel stations in the bus.

Ohhhh....I still feel guilty, and think of her often. After many phone calls and emails with the Blinman Mine

Tour Office over several weeks, I have had to accept that Sooty is gone from our lives.

Still, by all accounts, there have been many sightings in the weeks since she jumped ship; but although good-hearted people have tried traps and food and calling, she's gone native and seems to be happily roaming the night lands of the Flinders with her kindred feral cat friends.

So I imagine her living the life of a wild cat, with all its freedom and risks, and instead of a dusty old bus she has the wonders of the night sky, the quivering rustle of prey in the bush, her little ears alert; it may be a short life, but one that she lives with her senses and self unencumbered, a cat free to enjoy her catness.

But I miss her, and I hope that her journey's end, when it comes, is dignified, and that she is not afraid.

The Trek Begins

First things first - I stop to take the obligatory Nullarbor sign photo, then get roped into taking group shots for some German girls who want to stand on their car. A few hundred metres west of the sign that says "treeless plain" I see a tree.

I stop at the Head of the Bight tourist centre, which seems to sum up many things which are wrong with our modern world. Set among hundreds of kilometres of unfenced, uninhabited open land which looks out upon the thousands of kilometres of unbroken ocean horizons stretching away towards the vast unknown, you are made to drive through a gate and pay five dollars to see the

Great Australian Bight.   Before you get to the various signs providing scientific information about southern right whales and geography, you pass signs about Aboriginal creation myths, such as the "giant snake" that made the land. Each to their own, I suppose, as I move on quickly to the real stuff.

In the end the view from the Bight is pretty spectacular, and more importantly, there is a good selection of fridge magnets at the tourist shop.

Next stretch of the Nullarbor for Waggin 'Trail : Nullarbor Roadhouse to Mundrabilla. Hundreds of kilometres of nothinnnngggg.... I see two wild dingoes (beautiful) and a large black snake. I decide against bush camping out here with my beloved four-legged travelling companions.

After several hours of unchanging scenery I see we are almost at Border Village, where - this may come as a surprise - you cross the border into Western Australia.

At the border a cheerful quarantine officer relieves me of a jar of generic honey which, if I had been able to bring it into the state, could apparently have wiped out generations of sheep – at least that was the implication! So I wonder then, how they prevent the South Australian bees from crossing into Western Australia. Do they have swarms of Western Australian worker bees trained to be on border patrol, or what?

SCABS GO HOME!!

Mundrabilla: Middle Of Nowhere

When you see these places on the map you assume they are towns, but each one is just a desolate roadhouse with a gravel "caravan park", 1950's shower block and wildly expensive fridge magnets, or, if you really want to splash out, beer mats with cartoon pictures of three camels humping each other. That's if you have any sellable organs left after buying a litre of diesel.

These places are the remaining vestiges of early stations and camel routes; in the tired prefab buildings the brightly coloured souvenirs try to perpetuate some kind of garbled myth of Aussie outback spirit. The modern reality is a sausage factory of caravans and motorhomes grimly slogging from one petrol bowser to the next, through a landscape strewn with poison baits and truck-squashed kangaroos.

After the Nullarbor, the raggedy trees at Mundrabilla look like a verdant oasis. We gather for a good laugh as two of the other caravanners have a go at this stage of the Nullarbor golf course, watching them trying to actually find it in the scrub. I meet a prospector who has an awesome self-built off-road motorhome; he's off west again to look for gold.

Halfway Across

On to Eucla, where they have scenery and a bend in the road! I top up on diesel – the price is approximately $21.98 a litre plus a kidney and any valuables you may have in your vehicle.

Honey and I hike to the old Telegraph Station which is being swallowed by "the ageless sands of time". Smokey, shattered by an earlier nasty bird encounter, politely declines to join us. This proves to be a good decision on his part as we are suddenly swooped by a whole flock of stunning scarlet galahs. We walk to the ocean; it's turquoise, endless and wild.

At the Eucla rest stop, Smokey again attracts a small fan club, including a young motorcyclist who travels full time on his bike. He only works in order to save up and keep travelling – he has almost no gear packed on his bike and has one of the happiest faces I've ever seen.

I Google the Nullarbor weather radar for him to see if there's any rain coming his way from the east – even in the wild, I have not lost my production manager skills. I print out some hard copies and a quick call sheet and bingo! – he's on his way.

CHAPTER 11

January 2012: The Sporting Life

Tennis Anyone?

The last time I can remember playing any really serious tennis was when I was in college back in Britain. I was nineteen, training to be a teacher, and since one of my majors at the time was P.E. I was expected to master skills in a variety of common sports that were part of elementary and high school education at that time. These included rounders (a kind of baseball where you learn to catch a hard ball with your bare hands instead of some padded glove – considered to be wussy in British terms), soccer, gymnastics, field hockey, netball, track events and of course tennis.

Our women's P.E. instructor was a diminutive dynamo of a woman who must have been at least in her fifties. She was just over five feet tall, with short salt-and-pepper gray hair cut in what we considered in those days to be a very "butchy" style, and an elf-like face with a nose that appeared to have been broken at some point in time.

She was deadly serious about P.E. (it would be the saviour of civilization, was the implicit message) and rarely smiled. Her standards were high, along with her expectations of those who ventured unsuspectingly into her training course.

Heaven help you if you showed up not wearing the correct outfit for the sports lesson of the day. She herself never appeared wearing anything except tweedy knee-length shorts, navy blue jersey and thick lisle stockings.

Our own outfits were slightly less intimidating but still designed to protect us from the inclement British climate and the advances of any males who might be contemplating anything beyond cheering us on from the bleachers.

I think all of us in the women's group were intimidated by her, though in our final year, figuring there was safety in numbers, we undertook a collective protest by refusing to submit our hiking boots for her inspection prior to a day hike out on the local moors. In retaliation she cancelled the trip.

At the inevitable confrontation, she had come out of her bungalow and was standing between us and her goldfish pond. As the group launched me towards her to tell her that we were no longer school girls and objected to being treated as such, she took a disastrous step backwards, landing with one foot in the pond, narrowly missing a large startled Coi fish. We figured we had at least scored a tie. After a cooling off period, everyone pretended nothing had happened. Her repressed resentment, however, simmered until the next tennis session.

Rules and styles were different then. In those days we were not allowed to return a backhand in tennis with anything other than a single hand on the racquet. Following the fish-pond incident, out on the tennis courts several days later I instinctively – and I must say in this instance effectively - used two hands to return a backhand and was immediately hauled off the court for a verbal dressing-down by our perfectionist instructor.

Interrupting the game, she strode onto the court running her fingers dramatically through her short hair and shaking her head in disbelief. She stomped over, fixed me with her steely blue-eyed glare, and shouted loud enough for all to hear, "NO NO NO!! NEVER two hands on a backhand!!"

The British tend to be masters at public humiliation. They've had centuries of practice. I think she was actually disappointed that flogging was no longer permitted in educational establishments. Feeling duly demeaned in front of my peers, and quaking in my tennis shoes, I never again committed such a heinous crime – which of course drastically reduced my effectiveness against opponents. Wielding the heavy wooden racquet of the day, there was no way I could do a single-handed backhand.

Decades later, I wanted to call and tell her to turn on the tv and take a look at what was going on in Wimbledon, but sadly she was long-dead. She was only doing her best to prepare us for what was acceptable and correct for those times, I suppose. But I still felt somehow cheated out of what was obviously a natural strategy and is now considered perfectly normal and acceptable.

So it's only recently that I found the courage to take up tennis again. I'm not sure what brought it on. One day Peter and I found ourselves in a sports equipment store and bought a couple of cheapo racquets and a tube of balls. We were mesmerized by their colour – YELLOW! What sacrilege. I wondered what my college instructor would have had to say about THAT, along with the disappearance of the red cricket ball, now transformed to white! Is nothing sacred anymore?? Never mind. Go with the flow, *just do it* as the Nike mantra says. We've played more tennis in the last six months than ever before in our lives; but just the two of us playing singles. We wouldn't dream of inflicting ourselves on any other players.

At the resort, one day I see a notice about TENNIS ALL-PLAY that is routinely played every day except the weekends, in the late afternoon. I wonder what it means. I wander down to the courts to sit and watch.

It looks to be a sort of round-robin tennis. There are more players than places on the court, so you sit on the bench until someone calls out, "Player!", and then whoever is next in line joins the playing group as the last person to serve leaves the game and sits out. It looks incredibly democratic and non-elitist – this is, after all the USA. I have no idea what skill level is required, and I'm anxious that I'm going to be a complete liability to any foursome playing doubles.

Next day I look at the clock in the trailer with some trepidation – it's time. Racquet in hand, sunshade on head, I wander down to the tennis courts. Things are in full swing. Two courts are occupied with doubles players, with several people sitting on benches on the sidelines. I stand and watch from outside the entry gate. It doesn't look too bad. There's obviously quite a mix of ability levels, but nobody is out to kill and there's lots of encouragement all round, and good-natured humour. One pair is losing spectacularly, Love: 40. It's the final point in their game. They prepare for their last serve, and one of them says to his partner, "We're okay – we've got them exactly where we want them!" The ball slams into the net. "Game!" And everyone laughs.

"Come on in!" I hear somebody call out to me. I push open the gate and walk in.

"I'm Bill," he says. I tell him my name. "Hey, everyone," he says, and introduces me. Before I know it I'm paired up and ready to go.

"I'm not very good," I explain in good Canadian style, apologizing ahead of time for being a nuisance. "I'm 73 and can't run very fast anymore."

"Don't worry about it dahlin;," says Al, my opponent, "I'm 82 and not too swift either."

This lot are obviously not going to "go gentle into that good night"! There's going to be a substantial amount of raging against Dylan Thomas's "dying of the light."

My confidence starts to grow as I get instruction from my various partners, telling me where to stand and what to look out for and how to call the shots. I'm surprised how old some of the players are. I realize that the people here probably look younger because they're active – they move well, no shuffling around in this group. And in a game such as tennis, you have to *think* on your feet. It's a far cry from the Seniors' Fitness programme at the community centre back home where they sit on chairs, lifting one leg at a time, very slowly, and maybe doing a few arm curls; you'd get just as fit lifting teaspoons!

I find I'm really enjoying it, so I turn up to play over the next few days. After showing up for several days in a row, somebody asks me if I play for The League.

"League? What league?" I ask.

Turns out that the serious players are in a league that plays teams from other resorts and communities in the Mesa area, out in various parks. They sound committed and serious.

"You should try out for The League," a couple of the women tell me. "She's at least a 2.0, don't you think Sheila?"

"Oh she's better than that," says Sheila, "I'd put her at a 2.5 at least."

I have no idea what they're talking about. Is that good, so-so or what? Should I be signing up for Wimbledon? Should Serena Williams be worried? I wonder how high the ability numbers go – 20? 30? Here at the resort the highest ranking player seems to be a 4. I wonder what super players like Federer and Sharapova must be – in the 100s?

"They'll be doing trials for the league teams next week; you should sign up," they say encouragingly. Then, "How long are you here for?" And that's the let-down because I'm only here for another three weeks and The League want people who stay long-term. I find I'm a bit disappointed! I start wondering............

Meanwhile, Peter is tracking down his own preferred fitness mode: T'ai Chi. He's been doing it for a few years back home, up at the local community centre. It's taught by a couple of older women. The mood is calm, the movements are slow, meditative and flowing, with names like *Flying Stork Spreads Wings* and *Happy Cat Catches Butterfly*. It's all about keeping stress levels and blood pressure down and placing your feet carefully to maintain good balance. You wear whatever comfortable clothing suits you.

Here in Mesa Peter manages to track down a T'ai-Chi studio about a half-hour drive away. He calls ahead and talks to the young guy who is the instructor and who invites Peter to drop by and try one of the classes. A couple of days later Peter heads out to the studio.

The class is a group of young guys. They're wearing serious-looking black outfits trimmed in red. They don't appear to be particularly relaxed, but they make Peter welcome. The young instructor guy explains that the kind of T'ai-Chi he teaches is probably much faster-moving than what Peter is accustomed to. No matter. The lesson begins and yes, it's much faster and more aggressive than the classes back home; however, Peter notices that he completes the movements more fully than the young people and feels he has more flow. But he is not inclined to attend further classes in this particular style.

I meet up with him at the trailer after playing tennis.

75

"So," I say, "What did you learn at the T'ai-Chi class?" expecting to hear the usual meditation-happy-cat stuff.

"How to poke somebody's eyes out and break their arm," he answers.

It's at times like this that I wonder if the differences between men and women are not just to do with gender; I think we must be completely different species! Dear God! Poking out eyes and breaking limbs – for heaven's sakes!

We change into our swimsuits and shorts and stroll over to the swimming pools – the nicest, warmest we have ever been in; maybe they keep them warmer for old folks. We do a few lengths and then step into one of the Jacuzzis and set the bubble jets going.

Lounging back, enjoying the late afternoon rays of sunlight, I say lazily, " You know, I'm starting to really enjoy the tennis." Peter looks at me contemplatively. He knows intuitively what's going on in my head.

"So," – he asks, "do you think we should look at buying one of the trailers?".

Exactly.

CHAPTER 12

May 2011: Norseman - Esperance

Blow Out!

Five kilometres before Cocklebiddy, a rear tyre blows out on a cattle grid or something. A very kind young bloke at the roadhouse helps me change it. I am now travelling without a spare tyre. Run into the gold prospector again; he kindly offers to follow behind in case I have another flat. Unknown to me, the shuddering of the blowout has split another fuel line.

40 km out of Balladonia I catch an ominous whiff of diesel fumes. I make it to the Balladonia roadhouse and yep, sure enough, another split fuel line. Try to seal it up with gaffer tape, which works for approximately zero seconds. Wine, shower, bed. In the campground, two other motorhomers have their bonnets up; I'm not the only one with Nullarbor road ravages. Behind every roadhouse there are stacks of busted tyres and wrecked car parts. Isn't this fun!

The Price of Rescue

Well, it's going to cost $1000 but the tow truck is on its way; and after days of mind-numbing endless straight road and grey skies you would pay

anything to have

someone drive while you try to knock yourself out with whatever non-prescription drugs are in the bottom of the toiletry bag.

While I'm waiting, I go and look at the famous Skylab debris which is great. This space station was used for numerous experiments from 1973 until 1979 when its mission ended and it re-entered Earth's orbit. Most of it disintegrated but some parts fell in this remote part of Australia. Nothing and nobody was hurt.

Adam, the Indonesian tow truck driver, is lovely and we pass the time listening to his only CD: Michael Buble's Greatest Hits. He tells me how the Nullarbor is notorious for breakdowns. Many people end up camped out by their vehicles for days waiting for parts – I'm lucky. We reach Norseman, a small gold mining town past its use-by date at the western end of the Nullarbor. Motorhomers weeping with gratitude are staggering out of their RV's and kissing the $1.45 a litre price display at the local filling station.

Nullarbor

At first glimpse the town looks charming, but you soon realise most of the shops are abandoned. Through the dusty windows you swear you can glimpse the occasional skeleton of a shopkeeper. We arrive at the garage, greeted by mechanic Wayne, who has an angle grinder safety cover made of an old Arnott's biscuit tin.

Smokey is quite taken with the garage and moves into administration mode. When not directing people in distress to the office, he relaxes on the Ryco filters product shelf. Honey gets stuffed with snacks by Catherine, the shop manager

and is a big hit with the Aboriginal kids.

Half the town drops by the garage to chat – Elise, who rescues the town cats and dogs; Lois (Catherine's mum) who settles down for no reason in the office, and Sean, a nomadic motorhomer and the town's beekeeper, who offers me a spare paddock for the night. Again, people are terrific – Wayne offers me the use of the "troopy" 4WD, Catherine draws me a map, and everyone who passes by is invited to come and look at Smokey on the product shelf.

How to Catch a Chihuahua

So now Sean's dogs are slathering out the truck window at Honey, Smokey is sitting in the corridor of the garage office cleaning himself, I'm set up on the footpath with my camping table and laptop, various characters are wandering in and out patching up their vehicles while Wayne curses and groans from inside my bus, when the local animal ranger turns up to catch a tiny stray chihuahua which has just run past us.

No one has been able to get near the Chihuahua for weeks; it's starving and desperate, and Wayne's been leaving food out for it. Soon all the garage blokes are trying to surround the dog, tempting it with snacks, while the ranger tries to throw a net over it, with no success. They give up.

Now, I'm not clear on how this all happened, but a few hours later the Chihuahua is named "Sweetie" and is tucked up in bed with me and Honey, her tummy full, pressed up against me and sighing deeply as she finally stops trembling and falls asleep.

I lie there thinking that sometimes the best parts of a journey are when things go wrong.

Esperance

I'm now in Esperance, which as many of you will recollect is the birthplace of Esperanto. Aloh bugerhoff! as the friendly Esperantese say. Here for a couple of weeks of R & R after the horrors of the Nullarbor, staying in a very cute holiday unit by the beach. It is as beautiful as the tourist photos - azure sea, white sandy beaches, stunning.

Managed to give Sweetie the Chihuahua to Wayne the mechanic in Norseman thank God. So cute. He adores her and she has really taken to him so it's a very happy ending.

So far, for me the highlights of Esperance are not the stunning national parks or the azure waters – these things pale into insignificance compared to the fact that within one 300 metre stretch of the main road are the caravan supply store, an auto electrician, panel beater, UHF radio shop, gun shop and Bunnings.

At this Bunnings – brace yourself – people actually help you, and, amazingly, know where things are. One fellow (you may need to sit down to handle the shock here) actually showed me where something was, then – you'll think I'm making this up – CAME BACK to see if I wanted help carrying anything. These are the highlights you won't find on the tourist website.

For any of you who still think I am mad taking pets on the road with me, let me tell you about Adam. He was camped at Salmon Gums where I spent the night between Norseman and Esperance. As I parked, I could hear all this mad barking at the next campsite. Looking over, all I could see was a tent bulging and writhing as if it was about to hatch. I had to check it out!

Adam lives on the road full time doing casual work. He travels with FOUR DOGS. The dogs are called

Gorgeous, Adorable, Beautiful and Cobber - four mad farm dogs all the size of a border collie. Adam drives a ute, and all four dogs ride in the front seat with him because he doesn't want them falling off the back of the truck! At night they all squash into the small tent with him. Can you imagine?

Off to meet Sammy the Seal tomorrow. He lives at the Tanker Jetty here in Esperance in the crystal clear water. Little fish swim along beneath him, eating his sea lice. He doesn't have to go to work or learn how to use a mobile phone. People bring him fish and he has two lady seal friends. Don't you wish you could be a sea lion?

Ten Facts About Living In A Motorhome

1.   You don't miss work at all.
2.   You relax and doodle along, chatting with interesting strangers.
3.   You meet a lot of dogs.
4.   It's never boring.
5.   Everything in the motorhome smells like the dog.
6.   Organic lime air freshener does not work on dog smells.
7.   There are lots of amazing people living on the road.
8.   You can live with very few "things" (but lots of tools).
9.   You stop caring about TV.
10. You can make cups of tea for passersby in the car park.

CHAPTER 13

January 2012: To Buy Or Not To Buy

(That is the question)

The Decision.

For several days we toy with the idea of buying into the resort. We're still not sure – we haven't been here very long; there are still just over two weeks left of our holiday. The days trundle by; we're relaxed and fit; and surprisingly we've also been productive with our writing projects. It's a pleasant, stress-free routine. We tell ourselves we'll think about longer residency maybe when we get back home and have had time to get it into some kind of perspective. Very sensible.

Before we know it, we have only one week left. We raise the residency / purchasing question again, agree that we definitely should not act in haste, then turn on the TV just at the precise moment when it's showing the weather back in British Columbia. The pictures look like something from a Shackleton expedition – people in fur-trimmed hooded parkas, leaning against a wind that is whipping snow horizontally past the camera, temperatures in a minus degree range that have broken decades-old records. People are slipping and sliding around on ice-and-snow-covered sidewalks; semi trailer transport trucks lie tipped over and contorted in the ditches along the highways; shelters for homeless people cannot cope with the numbers; cars on black ice slide out of control and smash like bumper cars at a fairground into other vehicles parked on the street. It's like a preview for an apocalyptic disaster movie. We turn and look at each other in consternation, reach for the Units For Sale flyer on the kitchen table, and start making phone calls.

The Search

First thing next day, we take a walk round the whole complex, locating the units listed for sale. There seem to be quite a few. Somebody tells us that in these complexes there is usually about 10% of the units for sale. Although all have to conform to the 400 sq. ft. maxim, some people have opted for adding what is called an Arizona Room, but their size is also restricted.

We now start to notice the different brand names of the trailers. We see names like Cavco, Fleetwood, Redmon, Key Largo. They have slightly different floor plans and layouts. Adding an outdoor deck and storage shed seem to be the most common upgrades. Some people have added awnings and tinted UV film over the most sun-exposed windows. It's quite an education once you start really looking at details.

The prices range from high-end ($70,000 +) to insanely cheap ($14,000). Coming from Vancouver, where $70,000 would barely get you a garden shed to live in, we find the prices incredulous! All include furniture, bed linens, pots and pans, cutlery and appliances and more. We make a note of the ones we think might suit us, and contact a couple of people whose names and phone numbers are listed as being in charge of showing and selling the units on behalf of the owners : they are Bill and Joan.

They turn out to be very helpful, non-pushy people. They seem to do this job out of the kindness of their hearts, though hopefully they get some form of remuneration for their trouble. They also offer absentee services such as cleaning your unit before you return for the season, and watering and weeding the small area of garden connected with each unit while you're away. Good people.

It's a bit tricky to get in to see some units as they are occupied by seasonal renters, but we manage to visit a handful to get some idea of what the choices are. We check out a couple that already have an Arizona Room. They seem huge, and are several thousand dollars more. We're not sure if we need that much space. In the unit we are currently renting we only seem to use the Arizona Room for storing our luggage or going on the internet because that's where the connection is. We already have redundant space in our townhouse back home. Do we really need to start doing the same thing here? Hmmm.

We finally pick out a unit that seems to be a reasonable price and not as old as some of the others. But it is occupied by renters until the beginning of April, and they are not terribly happy at having people go in to look the place over. They don't answer the phone, and they mostly seem to be out during the day. Bill and Joan are unable to contact them to make an appointment, so we write a note and tape it to the front door, asking if we might come and look at it just for a five-minute walk-through. Then we sit and wait and keep our fingers crossed.

Next morning at 9 o'clock, our phone rings, and a man's gruff voice tells us that we can go and have a look at the place if we go RIGHT NOW. We slip on our shoes and sweaters and jog round to Bluebird Lane as fast as we can.

The man opens the sliding glass door to let us in. He seems less than happy. His wife is sitting at the small kitchen table reading. She looks up briefly and gives a shy smile. The man immediately flops down into a rather well-used dark blue velvet-covered reclining chair – the kind that seems to have a sort of gear-shift on the side (we have never cared for them).

We're also not very keen on the gauzy, flimsy tie-back curtains with their fussy valances. But the venetian blinds look okay. There are ornaments of course, but they can be easily disposed of. We try to visualize the place without all the clutter and kind of dressing-up we don't go for.

Part of the living room area is covered with old, pinkish-coloured, thick plush carpet. It's difficult to tell if the colour is by nature a sort of dusty rose, or if it's a twelve-year gradual wearing and discoloration that has given it a beating.

"THAT was FILTHY when we moved in," says the man in an accusatory tone, pointing to the plush carpet. His tone seems to imply that somehow it's our fault. The rest of the flooring seems to be rather old linoleum tile. So - furniture rather old and dated, and flooring not too good. However, the unit is light and bright. The cupboards and drawer fittings are of bleached oak veneer – and a feature that really appeals to us is the small computer nook with a pretty octagonal window. The bathroom has a full bath and shower and the toilet looks pretty new – and it's all very clean.

Outside there's a shed with a washer and dryer and some tools. We'd have to add our own deck – but there seem to be people around who do this as a regular job. Probably costs around $2000, so we've heard. The lot itself seems a bit smaller than some of the others we have looked at, and the landscaping is simple and not fussy. A citrus tree would be nice, but maybe we can plant one if we buy the place. There are rules about this too – about the kind of shrubs and cacti you can plant. As you walk around the narrow lanes you can understand why. Prickly pear, barrel cacti and other spine-bearing desert flora, can be quite hazardous in a tight community situation. We can see that people have had to remove the spines from some of their plants, to prevent injuries to passers-by. They've probably watched enough People's Court episodes to know what that can lead to.

We thank the renters for allowing us to visit, and go back to think this over. We like it. It needs some upgrading to make it to our taste, but we both liked how light and bright it is. It faces north-west, and there was no noise from outside traffic when we stood outside and listened. There's another house next to it on one side, and a trailer pad on the other, exactly like the place we're renting.

The owner is asking $21,900. We decide we'll make an offer of $19,000 and see how it goes. Bill and Joan come over to see what we're thinking. Turns out that the owner will pay the fees for the following year at the resort – an amount of $5000. This changes our offer – it's a good deal.

So we go for $21,000 which will still save us the $5000. Bill and Joan take the offer away with them and say they will contact the owner and get back to us as soon as possible; which turns out to be in the early afternoon. Our offer is accepted. We are delighted and excited.

Bank Strategy – Be Cheeky

Now we have to move into high gear because we have less than a week to deal with paperwork, registrations, and first and foremost getting cash for the deposit. This might be a problem. We don't have a bank account in America; we carry very little cash; we rely on Visa most of the time. We call our bank back in Canada – they can't wire the money quickly enough.

"What about using an ATM?" we ask.

Not a good idea they say; the denominations are too little and are doled out in $20 units, and there is a maximum you can withdraw; plus for every transaction we'd have to pay an extra fee, which would really add up with a $2000 withdrawal done in increments of $60 – $100. So how are we going to get $2000 before the day is out? We need to get the cash and open a bank account pronto. We decide we're just going to have to wing it and possibly be a bit cheeky. We jump in the car and drive to the bank we've seen in the Safeway supermarket. We'll just be truthful and brazen.

We wait in line at the bank counter until it's our turn. The name tag on the young fellow behind the counter identifies him as the Assistant Manager. We explain that we need $2000 cash for the deposit on a small house we're buying, and ask if he can advise us what to do.

ABM: "Do you have an account with us?"

Us: "No."

ABM: "But you're from Mesa or Phoenix, right?"

Us: "No. We're from Canada."

ABM: "Oh." Uneasy pause. Then: "I'm not sure about this. Let me ask my boss."

He waits for the bank manager to finish with another customer and then goes over and talks to him. They both look over at us and there is some discussion. We smile and try not to look like criminals, though we are aware of our new potential status as high-end alien trailer-dwellers.

The manager comes over. We have the same conversation as we did with the assistant except he doesn't say the bit about not being sure. Instead, after identifying ourselves as Canadian:

BM: "Have you got a bank credit card?"

Peter: "Yes."

BM: "Let me see it please." Peter hands it over.

BM: "I can give you a cash advance if you like. What's your card limit?"

It's plenty. The manager swipes it in his machine, tears off the receipt, goes into the vault and comes out with a fist full of $100 bills amounting to the required $2000! He counts it out for us, puts it in a secure envelope, hands it to Peter and then shakes our hands.

"Congratulations, and welcome to Mesa," he says.

The assistant comes over and does likewise, and tells us we can contact him any time if we need to know anything about Mesa and Phoenix.

"I don't go to bed until late, so you can even call me at home after bank hours if you need to," he says. Here we go again, we think – these people are unbelievable.

With our money stashed safely in a secret compartment of my purse, we head on over to Bill and Joan's house, which is not in the resort, but in another, non-gated but age-restricted community not far away. Joan goes to work immediately on the computer, coming up with a receipt, a print-out of what our property taxes will be, and a lot of paperwork that has already been completed with the business office at the resort. They don't just let anyone buy in. We have to pay for a background check.

Mandatory inspections have been completed but the unit needs to be registered at the motor vehicle department because it is classified as a vehicle. Of course, in the resort all these units have to be skirted so that the wheels cannot be seen. It adds a kind of psychological sense of permanence and enhances the appearance.

Just to be sure we know what we are getting into, Bill then produces a stack of colour photos showing what happened to the resort when it was hit by a terrible rain, hail and wind storm several years ago. It looks like a tsunami disaster area! Trailers torn off their pads with bent and twisted awnings totally wrecked, roads and gardens washed out and the whole place looking like one large lake. It's very alarming but doesn't put us off. But it does motivate us to get the place insured as soon as we can take ownership.

Next step is to get the trailer registered at the Motor Vehicle Department. It looks like a bit of a major undertaking – a forty-minute drive to the location and then a long wait in the lineup to get the registration. It can take the best part of a day. We're running short on time so we opt to pay Joan a small fee to do this for us using a proxy form. The form has to be witnessed and signed by a notary, so we head back to the bank for advice and find that – surprise, surprise – the bank manager is a licensed notary. He notarises the document and waives the normal fee charged for this service.

We've gone as far as we can with the purchase. We can't take possession until April 1st. It crosses our minds that, like Anna's starting point on her journey, it will be April Fool's Day.

CHAPTER 14

May 2011: Esperance - Perth

Feedin' A Hoss

Staying at a very cute farmstay place this weekend in Esperance as we finish off the motorhome upgrade. My job: feeding Pharus the very old horse. He's 32! The weather has been terrible (rain, cold, wind) so he got a double blanket coat to put on (well, we helped him put it on, he's not very handy with the buckles).

Drove along the Great Ocean Drive – sadly the weather doesn't do justice to the colours of the water and coast, but this would be a wonderful place to spend the summer months. Locals dancing for joy in the streets at the rain while we tourists race from one scenic lookout to the next, darting out to take a photo and saying "crikey it's cold" then hopping back in to bring up the next GPS scenic location directions.

Country Radio

Radio here achieves unsurpassed heights of local creative genius. Like TV, the ads are all for practical things that men like, and usually feature addictively catchy jingles like this:

> When yer paddock needs some fencin'
> Or yer cows just need a drenchin'
> And the pump's gone all to billy-o
> Just see the bloke from Rossie's
> He's a true blue dinkum Aussie
> For a brand new tractor, we're the factor,
> The men in your shed, we're Rossie's!

If you hear any radio ads with women in them, they're usually for mental health services.

Note in passing: We have been to Bunnings so many times that Honey just sits with the "meet 'n' greet" person at the front entrance without having to be told. The staff are planning to make her a little Bunnings jacket out of an old shop apron.

Hyden And The Wave Rock

Spent the last two days driving across the godforsaken wheat belt of middle WA, but I had to see Wave Rock at Hyden.

Dramatic moments near Hyden at sunset as I tried to turn the bus around on a nasty dirt track and somehow managed to lock it in third gear, right in the middle of nowhere. The clutch was stuck! I couldn't stop or I'd stall and not be able to get going again, so suddenly it was like that movie "Speed". I did a good job playing the role of Sandra Bullock; Honey was good as Keanu Reeves, Smokey was the calm guy with the headset back at base, and the demonic GPS played the role of Dennis Hopper, maniacally demanding insane sudden turns.

I got to a rest stop in Hyden (pop. 12), turned the engine off, googled "clutch stuck in gear" on the laptop, discovered that it's just a matter of pulling the clutch pedal up again, and fixed the problem. You can't keep a good production manager down! But it was a relief to get to the campsite and haul out one of the bottles of vodka from the hooch locker under the bed after all that I can tell you.

The Dog Cemetery

Corrigin in Western Australia is about 250 kms east of Perth. This town is crazy about dogs. I hear there's a dog cemetery which I HAVE to check out. They have an annual dog and ute competition (utes line up with dogs in the back), so of course the first person I come across to get directions to the dog cemetery is a farmer and his dog in a ute. The cemetery is a bit further along the highway.

I start off OK in the cemetery but "Bundy – RIP Little Mate" gets me all weepy, then I get to "Paddy – My Soul Mate" and let out a little sob, and when I get to "Loveable Old Bob" I go to pieces.

Thankfully there's little traffic on the highway, so I don't think anyone sees me hugging the dog statue sobbing "you're all good dogs!" and leaving some plastic flowers at its feet. I cry half the way to Brookton, hugging Honey too much (she just thought it was a good place to have a wee and a poo – well, why not? Dog lovers would understand).

Camel Safari

I've come from Esperance via Ravensthorpe, Lake King, Hyden, Corrigin, Brookton and now we're in some forest that the GPS has brought us to, where the camel farm is located, somewhere near Perth I think. There's no one here, it's dark and I'm camped next to some camels who are about 50 feet away from the bus. The night is eerie with the sound of them munching hay and making strange low frequency camel snoozing noises.

Next day I discover that camels are gentle, placid creatures and I just fall in love with them. Very tall. Very slooooowwwww. And they don't smell like anything! Just a bit woolly. Rebecca, the guide, lets me ride untethered which is quite a privilege. We amble through Kalamunda National Park while the camels munch on various protected plants along the way.

At the camel farm, Rebecca said they sometimes get people who come and train there for months and then go off travelling Australia by camel on their own, and today I came across Woody, a bloke about my age with his dog, Spot, also travelling and living in an old decrepit Mazda bus for years, happy as anything. All of which adds to my discoveries of people who just decide to take that first step out the front door. Inspiring!

Next stop Perth – the big city.

"Half Safe"

Half Safe is an amphibious jeep (yes! a JEEP) which Ben and Elinore Carlin took across the Atlantic and drove across the Sahara in the 1950's (google it and watch the ABC TV video on YouTube). It is a fantastic story. I found out it was stored at the über-posh Guildford Grammar School in
Perth so I just rang up and asked if I could see it, and was offered a private tour by the archivist!

I was allowed inside the jeep-boat and got to sit at the wheel of Half Safe in the SAME SEAT where Ben and Elsinore Carlin sat as they battled gigantic hurricane waves on the Atlantic over fifty years ago! This was mega-awesome as no one ever gets in Half Safe – but Rosemary the archivist said I was one of the few women who'd ever come to look at it and she had never met anyone so excited about it.

The first thing you notice is that Half Safe is TINY. Everything about it makes you think, "They must have been crazy!" You cannot imagine it even getting across a pond, let alone the Atlantic and then the Sahara. It would have been unbelievably cramped, not to mention deadly hot in the desert – it's basically just a metal box covered in layers of marine goop. And it would have wallowed like a sea cow, they must have heaved their guts out every minute of the way. I sat in the driver's seat and tried to imagine Elsinore looking out at the massive seas – she must have been incredibly brave.

One of the things I like about the story is it's one of those examples of people just deciding what they want to do and going out and doing it, no matter how crazy others think it is. It was also amazing to compare it to the "grey nomad" motorhomes and "must have" equipment lists and mod cons we have in our rigs now – Half Safe's radio was in a cardboard box on a shelf, and they towed their fuel cans on ropes from the back. Nowadays you wouldn't get safety permission to even drive it in a paddock.

CHAPTER 15

February - March 2012: The Waiting Game

Anticipation And Lots Of Patience

It's been what has seemed like a very long two months of waiting. Neighbours who are still there have kept in touch from Arizona. They've had a bit of a cold spell, they say – "It went below 20ºC for two days – we had to put sweaters on!" We respond unsympathetically and continue to cross the days off the calendar.

Time comes to make the final payment on what will be our new holiday home. Although we don't need to wire the money until the end of the month, we decide to start the procedure a week early, just in case. Which turns out to be the right decision.

Bill and Joan send us the bank-wire instructions via the internet. The most critical component is the routing number, which directs the money to the account it is to be transferred to. We go to our bank and give them the details we have received, and transfer the appropriate amount to our US account for ease of transaction. All seems well. For half a day.

Then our bank calls to tell us the wire has been returned. The routing number is incorrect. Urgent calls to Bill and Joan, and from them to the owners who are dairy farmers in Iowa. The owners insist the information is correct; Bill and Joan advise us to give it another go. We think not. If our bank has tried and failed, then something is amiss.

First we call the bank that is supposed to be receiving and forwarding the wire in the US. It's a farmers' credit union. They say they only deal with people who have accounts in their credit union, and do not offer a forwarding service to a smaller bank with less status. They have nothing to do with the even smaller credit union where the current trailer owners have their account.

Next we call the owners' bank. It's another, smaller farming credit union. By now we imagine a small bank like the ones that are regularly held up at gun point in westerns, another candidate for a *Twilight* Zone episode: wood-frame building, standing on the street corner of some small isolated town, where the manager – wearing the traditional green shade visor – is walking around in shirt-sleeves held up with black elasticized bands, a watch chain dangling from his waistcoat pocket, a large ring of security keys in his hand as he pushes through the swinging gate to go and crank up the phone.

However, it's a female voice that takes our call. As we suspected, the small credit union does not have sufficient status to qualify for a direct wire; the routing number the trailer owners gave us is incorrect, and it has to be rerouted through another, more institutionally established bank.

Back we go to our bank with the new information. They decide to call the Iowa credit union again, just to be sure this time that everything will go through. It's a more complex process than the owners realized.

We get our grocery shopping done while the bank deals with the nuances of Iowa farming credit unions. When we go back, it's all done – we hope. We notify Bill and Joan again by email. Then everyone waits with bated breath and fingers crossed as we try to get the money transferred to the country that was able to put men on the moon back in the 70's but can't seem to get money into a small bank in Iowa in 2012.

Our bank in Canada tells us the transfer could take up to two days to get there. But miracle of miracles – in the late afternoon of the same day, we get an ecstatic email from Bill and Joan – the owners have received the money in their bank account. High fives all round – there *is* a God after all! Good job we got it sorted out before we hit the road south!

A few days before we leave we get a phone call from my son in Oregon to see how we're doing. He knew we were thinking of buying a trailer home. I tell him we're fine and that things are moving along nicely. Then I ask what's happening in his part of the world with him and his wife.

"Fine Mum," he says. "We sold our house in the subdivision and have bought a little old house that we're going to renovate inside and out – it's going to take some time."

I ask him where they are living in the meantime.

"In a little trailer," he says. "We really like it."

Is it something in the water or our family genes??

March 31st finally arrives. The people renting what is now "our" trailer have to vacate next day. We are packed and ready with new dishes, bed linen and a collection of household items we think we might need, not forgetting tennis racquets, hiking gear and swimsuits. We set out early and head south to the sun – at last!

CHAPTER 16

May – June 2011: Lancelin – Geraldton

Tourist Attraction : Dead Whale

The Indian Ocean and Western Australia (WA) coast at last! The caravan park is right by the beach, there's no one else here except Leon the sheep shearer and his working dog Nigel, who are running the park during non-sheep season, and when the ginormous huge rain storm that is covering all of WA goes away I expect to be frolicking in the warm sea with the local dolphins

It was sunset as I checked in. Normally they give you a little map and tell you where the toilet block is etc, but Leon is far more interesting. First he showed me the fish soup he's making in the back kitchen, then we looked at photos of the fish, then some photos of the bigger fish his dad caught. However, this was all just a preamble to the highlight feature of the caravan park, which is that there is a dead whale on the beach.

"If you go now, you should have just enough light left to see it!" said Leon.

Needing no further encouragement, I quickly set off, with Nigel the sheepdog rounding us up and leading the way (Nigel is bored as there are no sheep). Sadly it was quite dark when we finally found part of the dead whale (its head) rolling around in the heavy storm surf so I wasn't able to get photos. Thank goodness the dogs didn't roll in it, but hey there's always tomorrow...

Signs Of The Times – Lots Of 'Em

From Lancelin we came through Cervantes and Jurien Bay, spent the night at beautiful Sandy Cape campground, with a detour en route to the famous Wedge Island shack community.

Something I notice about WA is they are very keen on signs. There are signs everywhere telling you not to do things that would never occur to you until you read them on a sign. "No Camping – Offenders Will Be Hanged As Per Town Bylaw No. 28,753" and "Unregistered Vehicles or Drivers Will Be Confiscated and Cast Into the Sea" type signs everywhere, even in unlikely places such as behind the liquor store! Each of these signs has more signs nailed above, below and around it with fine print detailing various additional rules, punishments and heavily worded excerpts from local bylaws, followed by "Have a Great Visit!" cheerfully scribbled below.

In most places you don't even need to bring a holiday book, you can spend hours just reading all the signs. Presumably without all these signs people would just run amok, looting and burning everything in sight before hammering tent pegs into the car park in front of the grocery store for the night.

We stop at Sandy Cape for the night, a lovely spot (allow 2 hours to read signs at entry point) where we are sheltered from the howling gales and rain and Smokey (sole feline member of the Royal Geographic Society) and I go for an expeditionary walk on the amazing sand dunes. The dolphins who normally frolic in the bay have all nicked off to Central Australia to keep warm!

Cliff Head

If you decide to stay at the south end of the north section of the Cliff Head camp site, which is a large grassy area, you better be darn serious about grey nomading.

Don't even think of going in there with your crappy Wicked campervan, or try to palm yourself off as a longtimer if you don't have your matching recliner chair and table set. This is where I find "Denim N Lace", which is a doubledecker gigantic bus monstrosity towing a huge boxed car trailer. Remember that thing Robert Dinero drives in *"Meet the Fokkers"*? It's bigger than that. It has TWO STOREYS.

But everyone here is really nice and there's lots of socialising, mostly about our various travel experiences and equipment, and where we're heading next. There are mutterings about Broome; everyone is fed up with the unexpected rain and cold that's been dogging us all since Adelaide.

The men can be really funny. No matter where you say you went or where you say you're thinking of going, it's wrong. "Nah, you don't wanna go there. Go to blah blah woop woop, great fishin." I'll mention some other place and get "Nah! No fishin' there. Maybe some crabbin'. You wanna go to blahdyblah, we stayed there for a month. Crabs everywhere. Filled the freezer." ....Anyway you get the idea.

Geraldton Highlights

Geraldton is the last outpost of civilisation before we start the serious snorkelling/dolphin/camping part of this adventure in north Western Australia, so we're stocking up on gas, water, clutch spare parts and of course Bunnings stuff. I discover with joy that there is a Bunnings AND a BCF (Boating, Camping & Fishing) store right next to each other!!!

Somehow at BCF I managed to buy a whole bunch of squid and fish catching gear. The $20 Barbie Fishin' Grrl rod will struggle with the marlin but as Ernest Hemingway would put it, it's not the fish, it's the fight. I got a few raised eyebrows when I asked how to kill squid and crabs humanely. The store went kind of quiet like in a gunslinger movie bar scene so I quickly escaped to the tent section.

While the bus is having a preflight checkup with Eric the mechanic, my travelling companions and I will be living in our new groovy big tent at the caravan park, trying to assemble the fishing louvres or gromlets or whatever they are. The tent will be handy when I have visitors too. I bought it solely on the basis that it is a cheerful colour and has an Acrimony Assembly Rating of 3 (10 being homicidal rage).

The weather is unseasonably cold but at least it's sunny; fingers crossed it's good for Monkey Mia. The damn dolphins have probably gone to Bali or something.

Getting dark – the traditional time for assembling a new tent for the first time. Campin' fun!

CHAPTER 17

March 2012: Journey To Possession 1

Day 1: Vancouver, BC - Roseburg, Oregon

March 31st. and it's pouring with rain. Temperatures still struggling unsuccessfully to reach double figures. We set out at 7 a.m. to get to the US border early. It's a Saturday and the traffic shouldn't be too bad on the I-5.

The I-5 is the major highway linking North America and Mexico. After that it joins other major highways that continue down into South America. If you wanted to, and really put your mind to it and kept a handy supply of Valium, you could probably get all the way to the southern tip of Chile. Amazing.

Of course driving the I-5 can be a nightmare of semi-trailers hauling goods from the Pacific seaports to their big-box destinations, feeding the insatiable consumer appetites evident in the likes of Wal-Mart, Target, Home Depot. This morning though, it's pretty quiet and remains that way until we reach the Seattle suburbs, where the usual madness starts.

The weather gets worse and we find ourselves driving through sleet, worrying that maybe we have been a bit premature in deciding to remove our winter tires in exchange for the summer ones. We chose the route closest to the coast to avoid the spring snows of the more inland mountain passes, but this is not looking good for our destination of the day – Grants Pass, Oregon. The weather forecasters had offered clouds and rain with no mention of snow, but you sometimes wonder if they ever bother to look out the window to see what is really happening.

We make good use of the intermittent Rest Areas which are a boon to the highway travellers. Here people stop to take a nap, have a snack from a dispensing machine, let the kids out to run off all their pent-up energy, and give the dog a bathroom break in the specially designated area. A number of the Rest Areas have a small concession booth run by local volunteers who serve free coffee and cookies to help keep drivers alert and the accident rate down. They always seem to be cheerful, friendly folk, doing good work for their local communities – another good side of America that will never make the evening international news.

Following the highway south from Centralia, through Longview, the broad expanse of the Columbia River shows up on our right, eventually forming the border between Washington State and Oregon. It is a massive river.

After five hours, and right on schedule, we reach Portland and meet up for lunch with son Calvin and his wife Tracy. Their usual smugness at the superiority of their weather compared to ours in White Rock, is no more. They are wearing fleece jackets, gloves and warm toques. We have a one-hour catch-up on news, eating lunch at a Thai restaurant, and then they guide us back onto our route south, envious of our warm destination and requesting invitations for a visit when we're all set up in Arizona.

For a while we follow the I-205 which takes us through Salem. It's a quieter highway. The sun puts in a brief appearance and then it's back to several downpours.

We travel through pretty, rolling country with scattered sheep farms. The hills and animals remind us of New Zealand. Some blossoms and a few daffodils are making a bold attempt to put on a show, but it's obvious that spring is on indefinite hold for now. There is evidence of recent flooding. A desperate sign in a totally water-logged field states: FILL WANTED. *You don't say!*

Peter spots many hawks wheeling above us as we drive along.

"Look! That's a turkey vulture!" he calls out.

Afraid to take my eyes off the road for more than a nanosecond I ask him, as I often do,

"How can you tell?"

"They have a red face," he says. How does he do it, without even having full binocular vision (due to a childhood accident involving a glass display case in a store).

He and my daughter Anna are keen bird spotters, and when we get the chance to spend time together travelling and hiking, they are always at the ready with binoculars slung around their necks. They seem able to recognize even the smallest identifying features.

A bird will flash by in the middle of some tropical island forest, and they'll say, "It was a yellow-bellied sapsucker," or something. As for me, I'm aware that something has gone swooping by but the most I'm able to come up with is along the lines of, "It was big/ small/ brown/ grey," or "That was a bird."

So my standard question is always the same – "How could you tell?" Then they say something along the lines of, "You could see it had a small red dot just below its eye." It drives me insane. How do they do it? Sometimes I think they must be making it up just to make me feel inadequate. But no – that's not it because later when we've returned to our residence, out come the bird books for reference, and the wretched Sapsucker or whatever will be there on page 49, red dots and all.

Another five hours of shared driving brings us to our destination of the day, just about 100 kms short of Grants Pass, the small town of Roseburg. Ten hours of driving is enough at our age. Any more than that, and with the onset of darkness, we worry about becoming a hazard. We have also determined to make the long journey part of the adventure – we shall see a lot of the US. It's an amazing country.

The small motel is adequate. The only place nearby to get food is a Quiznos sandwich shop. It will do – the food is fresh and tasty. Peter walks over to buy us sandwiches.

Just as he turns the corner from the motel, a police car pulls up outside the Quiznos, lights flashing. The officers jump out and go inside. Peter keeps a safe distance. You never know these days if there is a hold-up going on, a shoot-out, or even if it's all part of some movie-making enterprise.

The officers come back out, get into the squad car and drive off.

"What do you think was going on?" I ask Peter.

"I don't know," he says. "Perhaps they were *really* hungry and needed fast service."

The weather remains cold and wet. A young couple who checked into the motel just ahead of us described a horror story about trying to get through the mountain pass which was covered in snow! We wonder what's in store for us tomorrow morning – seems like we should have left the snow tires on the car. Too late now. Nothing is going to get much better or warmer until we start heading down from the mountains and into California.

CHAPTER 18

June 2011: Geraldton – Carnarvon

Stromatolites

The day before yesterday I was camped at Coronation Beach with the usual grey nomad pack when another old bus pulled up into the last campsite, next to mine. Jeff, who's about my age, hops out with his dog Gooch and soon both dogs are in each other's buses and we're having a great time.

I won't go into detail about how Jeff makes a living on the road but let's just say that Gooch is short for "Gucci" and there is shag carpet and a lot of umm, interesting costumes in his bus. He is great company, kind, happy and very funny, so we decide to "tagalong" with each other on the road next day to Monkey Mia.

We arrive at Hamelin Pool, a side detour in order to see the Amazing Ancient Stromatolites, which from a bit of research and encouragement from family members who have been here before, are apparently Not To Be Missed. For what it's worth, here is the lowdown on this fascinating highlight – if it's your kind of thing:

Everybody keep perfectly still!

Stromatolites are ancient rocky accumulations that date back over three billion years. They are found in several countries. What is special about the ones at Hamelin Pool and Shark Bay in Australia, is that THEY ARE STILL ALIVE AND GROWING (aaayyeeeee!!). They provide the scientists who get excited about this kind of thing, a fossil record of what passed for "Life" in those distant times. The ones that are still what might laughingly be called "active" have managed to survive due to their salt-water environment. The onset of grazing animals seems to be the explanation for the decline in stromatolite numbers in other places. The ones that appear to still be growing are the oldest life forms on earth, making the biblical Methuselah look like a baby in diapers at a purported age of 969.

Anyhow, we check out the stromatolite viewing area and are awed and amazed at the prehistoric wonder…..for about five minutes, then we go and check into our overnight spots at the charming Hamelin Pool campground, which is kind of like the Benny Hill show without the music.

Several guests appear to be trapped there working to help out the manager, and from the chaos emerges Dave, the mad diesel mechanic, roo shooter and handyman who wastes no time in wooing me with fresh kangaroo steaks. "We don't get many single women out here! Please come back soon!" We make plans to meet up in Carnarvon for some fishing, but in the meantime the dolphins are calling.

Monkey Mia

Shark Bay at Monkey Mia is INCREDIBLE! Monkey Mia is the most westerly point of Australia. This is the spot where, several years ago, Mum, Peter and Ben had rented one of the shoreline cottages in order to get a clear view of the dolphins coming in for their intermittent visits with humans. The story has it that on arrival, the three family members had merrily run down the beach and into the sea to splash around in blissful ignorance, to cool off. In the evening they attended an educational talk by one of the Ph.D. students working at the research centre (he happened to be Canadian) – and that's when they found out why it's called Shark Bay: just about every known species of shark either inhabits or visits the bay!! Good grief! Suddenly they could all three recall really clearly the theme music from "Jaws" --- no more blissful splashing around after that.

The dolphins at Monkey Mia are of course famous for what people perceive to be their friendliness towards the humans who wait patiently each day for their arrival at the shoreline. The rangers at this protected World Heritage Site (on account of the huge beds of sea-grass, not the dolphins) claim that they (the dolphins, and come to think of it, quite possibly the rangers too) are not being habituated by the handouts of fresh fish. This may or may not be true, depending on your point of view. The dolphins only receive what is claimed to be 10% of their necessary daily intake, and the supply does seem well controlled. When tourists have distributed the couple of buckets of fish to the dolphins, that's it. The dolphins know it's over and head out back to sea.

Whatever the ethics of the scene, it is truly wonderful to see the dark dorsal fins appear way off in the distance, leaping their way to rendezvous with the humans quietly awaiting them in shallow water close to shore.

The dolphins that visit appear to be exclusively female, and they bring their babies with them. Few experiences can match the feel of a small torpedo body brushing past your legs in the water, turning on its side to look up at you and quickly taking the fish from your hand. You have to be on your best behaviour of course. There are strict rules. You are allowed to stroke the dolphins along their sides, but you must never touch their blow-hole. In

The Trailer Diaries

terms of interacting with wild animals it's the stuff of dreams.

Jeff gets us a great ocean view site, so-called because if the five hundred other caravans and campers weren't jammed in there you could probably see part of the bay.

After a not-so-exciting dolphin "encounter" in a freezing cold wind the next morning, we flee the sardine-can campground of Monkey Mia. Jeff continues on to Exmouth while I head for Coral Bay to play with the manta rays.

Things slowly begin to get wonderfully chaotic; little do I know it, but I'm getting my first taste of Western Australia's "see how it goes" lifestyle. Coral Bay is nice but too touristy and the coral reefs are badly damaged, so I go back to Shark Bay and spend a week fishing out of Denham with Dave, who's brought his tinny (small boat).

Dolphins play about the bow of the little boat, so close I can touch them, and we're surrounded by turtles and reef sharks – it's beautiful. Each night we head down to the Denham jetty to try and catch the elusive squid. Smokey and Honey follow us through the small town, much to the amusement of the locals. Smokey strolls the pier, inspecting each person's catch. "I think he wants his own rod," smiles one of the fishing blokes.

After a week of wandering around barefoot and living on fish I decide it's time to keep heading north. I leave Dave distraught at Hamelin Pool ("Stay here! I'll get you a baby camel! A boat! Anything!") and point the bus towards Carnarvon.

Carnarvon

After a very long and straight 230 km drive which feels exactly like the Nullarbor, I get to Carnarvon. This is the place where Robyn Davidson of "Tracks" fame (a great read) ended her one-woman 1700 mile trek across the deserts of Western Australia with her camels.

It's a funny little place with a population of about 6000 people - a mix of aboriginal, "white", Vietnamese and Pacific islander people. Among themselves, my perception is that the whiteys use a lot of racist language and have a low opinion of non-whites, especially aboriginals. I am shocked at how often I hear the word "coon" used here.

On the surface, relations between the various groups are friendly enough and on an individual basis people seem fine with each other. But you rarely see whites mix on a social level with non-whites, and "interracial" couples are rare. The town seems very class conscious, which seems ridiculous in such a small population in the middle of nowhere, but there you go.

There are palm trees, frangipani, bougainvillea - you can tell you've crossed into the tropics. Lovely fresh local fruit and vegetables – a roadrunner's dream after miles of expensive wilted truck produce. It's pretty, but at night while the caravan campers are securely locked up behind high fences in the caravan park, the town seems to go feral. There's a kind of wild west enthusiasm for "gettin' inta trouble" and so far it appears that I could be the only person in town who is not a professional roo shooter.

So I'm not wild about Carnarvon as a place, but the children here seem delightful. All of them are mad about fishing and offer me bait or fish, and want to ask me all kinds of questions. They seem to be out rambling around all day with just their fishing gear, so I end up sharing any fruit and snacks I've got (they're always hungry). The aboriginal children are real characters, and are obsessed with Honey.

Dave turns up and takes me out for an all-you-can-eat Homer Simpson seafood buffet. The bus is a bit cramped with the two of us plus Honey (who snores at night) and Smokey (who likes to sleep on my head) so we resort to a park cabin for the rest of the weekend.

The bus freezer and all our eskys (coolers) are full of our fish after a fantastic day of fishing on the huge One Mile Jetty – I'll never have to shop again!

CHAPTER 19

April 2012: Journey To Possession 2

Roseburg (Oregon),
to Merced (California)

We set out early again. The roads are wet, but at least it's not raining. There are some steep mountain passes to get under our belts today, but hopefully, once they're done we shall be able to wear at least one clothing layer less. But not right at the start. It's obvious from the drifts at the roadsides that it has snowed during the night, and the snow plows have been out good and early to keep this main traffic and transport artery open.

The mountain passes are high, with Siskiyou Pass reaching an elevation of over 4000 feet. When the sun comes out and the skies clear from time to time, we see the incredible vistas of endless alpine valleys, forests and snow-capped peaks. Then - we enter California.

Mount Shasta Pit Stop

Ahead of us Mount Shasta looms with its distinctive cone, the last (or first, depending on the direction you're heading) of the major volcanoes in the Cascade chain. We've driven by them all on this trip, but due to the inclement weather Shasta is the only one that has been visible.

Checking in at just over 14,000 feet, and part of the Pacific Ring of Fire, it looks massive. The lower slopes seem to reach almost to the edge of the highway. In the sunshine it looks as if it would be a straightforward hike up to the summit, but these mountains are notorious for their deception, some claiming several lives a year, mostly so-called experienced mountaineers seduced by the seemingly easy ascent, only to be caught short of supplies and equipment in a sudden, unanticipated snowstorm, with fatal consequences.

We take advantage of the Rest Area with its spectacular view of the mountain. Tourists and truckers alike pull in for a washroom and snack break. The trucks plying these highways are huge monsters. You wonder if anyone has ever bothered to study the stress levels of their drivers negotiating the vast distances they seem able to handle. No wimpy ten-hour shifts for these guys, and no overnights in hotels with turn-down sheets and chocolates on the pillow. Their bedroom is the space above the cab of the truck. They are the unsung heroes of any thriving economy.

A Trailer To Vegas

I'm washing my hands in the rest room when the older woman standing at the basin next to me asks in a loud voice,

"Which direction ya headin'?"

She's big, looks tough and isn't smiling.

"South," I say, and smile to show I'm friendly and she doesn't need to shoot me or anything, this being America and all. We've had some interesting cultural experiences on bike rides, passing through small-town America. Buying chips at a run-down tavern one time (it was the only place offering anything to eat or drink), we sat staring at the posters on the wall behind the bar.

"Gun control means having a steady hand" said one; another admonished customers to "Fight crime! Shoot back!" So we don't want to go upsetting the locals in remote places.

"South," I say again.

"I know THAT," she says, in a tone that implies I'm an idiot. On reflection, it is of course the only direction anyone can be heading if they've pulled into this rest stop – you can't access it if you're heading north; you have to wait for a north-bound rest stop to come up. Silly me.

"Where ya HEADED?" my washbasin neighbour valiantly persists, applying the commonly-used strategy when dealing with foreigners : *When in doubt, SHOUT.*

"Oh," I say, realizing that by *direction* she actually means *destination*.

"Mesa, Arizona." And then, because she's really dying for me to ask, I say, "How about you?"

"Goin' to LAS VEGAS," she says with a big smile. "Pullin' a trailer. Gonna be staying there TWO WHOLE WEEKS! Never bin there before."

I say it sounds fantastic, which, having been there myself, is true. Fantastic in the sense that if you ever want to see what hell will be like if you end up in the big casino in the sky, Las Vegas is the place to go.

"Have fun," I say. "Drive safely."

"Ya HAVE to when yer haulin' a TRAILER," she shouts, and stomps out. I can visualize the speech bubble above her head : *Stupid Canadians.*

For her it may well be the trip of a lifetime and she really will have fun, holding down expenses by living in her little trailer, playing blackjack and the slot machines in the casinos. It takes all kinds. And here's the irony –

in what was once (and possibly still is) regarded as Sin City with the promise of Sodom and Gomorrah combined, our trailer-towing lady will be *totally safe!*

From my own memories of the place, all the hotels and casinos in Vegas hire security agents who look like something out of a CIA documentary. Suits on wires. Everywhere. They operate unobtrusively but are there as soon as someone starts to be a nuisance – a happy gambler who's had too much to drink for example, and is starting to interfere with other people's fun. The suits appear out of nowhere and are extremely polite as the offender is firmly escorted away ("Please come with us, sir,"). I wonder if maybe they're suited-up clones of The Borg, like in the *Star Trek Voyager* movies, because resistance sure looks futile.

They're there to be helpful too though. Finding myself disoriented one time by flashing slot machines and video screens, and standing looking dazed I guess, a suit appeared and asked if I needed help. So it's not all about being hauled off to be tortured or brainwashed into understanding the niceties of public, acceptable behaviour – though when you watch the nightly news from elsewhere you start thinking that such alternatives might not be such a bad idea!

But Vegas is sort of Corporate Central where rules are rules and there's no discussion surrounding their enforcement, and you will *not* be provided with a psychologist to argue in court that you suffer from Attention Deficit. You either behave or go home. That's IT. And of course if you win an obscene amount of money (rare, because as the bus driver taking us to our hotel pointed out, "Vegas was not built on winners") you get your own security guards escorting you to your room – or possibly your trailer in the case of our enthusiastic lady at the rest stop. I hope she has a great time and doesn't lose the truck and trailer to Blackjack.

A Dinner at a Diner

We leave the southbound rest stop, begin the descent from the mountains and are again in New Zealand-like countryside. And it's getting warmer – at last! We continue south, the land now getting flatter with vast stretches of cultivated crops: vegetables, nuts, apple orchards, berries. Down through Williams and Dunnigall, skirting Sacramento, the state capitol.

We decide to make Merced our second stop of the journey and check into a motel where we bathe and change into summer clothes – yaaay! Beside the motel is a small restaurant. We check out the menu. It's similar to the ABC and Country Inn restaurants we know back home – has everything you could possibly want, plus a cheaper seniors' menu that is usually a sensible, appropriately-sized meal as opposed to the overlapping-the-plate, heart-attack-in-a-meal common in many places these days..

Part of the restaurant - the long sit-at-the-counter diner part – has been newly renovated. Its original '50's style now looks very sharp with a marble counter-top and new furniture, and is immaculately laid out ready for service. The other part is your traditional booth style with rather worn, fake leather-upholstered bench seating. But it's all clean and friendly.

We opt for a booth and have a pleasant, reasonably-priced meal. At the checkout, we chat with the owner – a big man with the requisite contemporary tattoos, wearing a chef's apron and baseball cap. Yes, the renovations were just completed last week and he's very proud of his business and hoping it will attract a larger clientele.

People work hard in the US, trying to overcome what they have recently had to go through with the recession that has led so many of them into loss of homes, loss of livelihoods and bankruptcy. They have a special kind of resilience that seems unique to the American culture and the belief of many people that problems can be overcome by sheer hard work and determination. A social welfare state does not appear to be in the works any time soon in America. It doesn't seem to be an ethos they aspire to. Coming from a reasonably socialist country, we can see the pros and cons of both sides. These days people seem to be falling through the cracks no matter what kind of system predominates. Maybe a return to so-called rugged individualism will be our only recourse in the end!

CHAPTER 20

July 2011: Time Out

The Roadhouse

I could write a whole novel about how I ended up working at a roadhouse 400 kilometres from anywhere, but let's just say that I somehow find myself shacked up with Dave the diesel mechanic in a compound of dongers (single person's accommodation, also called "dogboxes"), cleaning the shower block and running the roadhouse laundry in exchange for free food and a room.

I discover the relaxing pleasures of cleaning, but my past skills as a ferociously organised production manager are soon awakened - within three days, all the towels are colour coded and the bed linen is stacked in pre-assembled sets according to bed size.

Barry, the owner/manager of the roadhouse, has agreed to pay me $15 cash per room-clean for the motel rooms and – I can barely contain my excitement – he is going to take my advice and order colour-separated double and single bed linen sets to avoid the current confusion and chaos. The room cleaning only takes about an hour or two each day and is completely free of stress, unwanted phone calls, and emails.

Living at the roadhouse is sort of like being in an open-air communal camp, or possibly a detention centre, but with more laughs. Behind my "dogbox" there is a covered carport thing; the bus is parked alongside it, and I've turned the carport into an open air cantina with party lights and chairs so it's a cool hangout and my little private area.

In the mornings I wander into the kitchen and have breakfast in the restaurant area, then go off to do my chores. It's fun in the late afternoon or evening to just hang out in the kitchen or the public TV area and help a bit with the dishes or share a joke with the truckies.

Smokey comes for a stroll in the mornings around the staff area and seems quite pleased with the arrangement. He also likes to accompany me as I clean the guest rooms to make sure the cleaning and bedding arrangements are to his liking. He is quite fond of room 5 for some reason and I have to check each day that he's not sleeping in the beds!

There's the usual handful of outback Aussie characters passing through, picking up supplies and exchanging stories and information. Today's featured nomad is Conrad, who is pushing a wheelbarrow across Australia for a teen suicide-prevention charity.

Only 7546 more kilometres to go !

The wheelbarrow has solar power for his phone, a 25 litre water jerry, a 12 volt inverter and carries his swag and clothes. Today he is resting his battered feet – he started from Steep Point and is trying to do 35 km per day. Quite a feat (no pun intended).

Meanwhile, I've already had time to start on the Waggin' Trail repaint. It attracts the attention of both humans and animals, and at one point an emu dropped by with two chicks to offer some advice. Japanese tourists come and take photos.

Short-order Cookin'

Dave and I go fishing for a few days up at Warroora Station and return to discover that two of the part-time roadhouse girls have disappeared (voluntarily, we assume) with a departing roadwork crew and the two new women are starting to cave in under the long days......this weekend we are down to three of us running the roadhouse, which is insane. We tried to kidnap a passing electrician ("Can you cook?") but were unsuccessful. My suggestion is to make foreign backpackers hand over their passports when buying fuel, then hold them hostage as dish-pigs and toilet cleaners, sort of like the Eagles song *Hotel California* .... *You can check out any time you like, but you can never leave.......*

During the day all sorts of people and vehicles arrive - huge road trains with three or four trailers, the usual motley groups of caravanners and backpackers, and quite often someone unusual like the wheelbarrow guy, a cyclist or, as we got yesterday, some grey nomads using farm tractors to tow their caravans around Australia. Every once in a while you hear one of the staff yell out "BUS!!", which means that dozens of people are about to emerge from the Greyhound transit bus to wreak carnage in the toilets and eat twice their body weight in sausage rolls.

The roadhouse currently being in emergency mode, I am assigned to taking over some of the meal preparation. So after five minutes of intensive training I am feeling I can compete with even the best short order cook within 500 kilometres! I turn out a ton of burgers, steak sangas and mixed grill (gross pile of fat-oozing deep-fried meat) with a couple of coffee breaks out the back of the kitchen, gazing at the cockroaches dancing in the moonlight next to the empty fryer fat buckets.

Being the short order cook is fun because I take the meals out to the customers and get to catch up on the local road gossip, which is how I discovered that Conrad the Wheelbarrow Man made it to the Billabong Roadhouse (about 100 km away), then got a flat tyre! So he's waiting there for a new tyre to be delivered (why wasn't he carrying a spare?).

After a week or so, the rain starts up again making the weather very hot and humid. You'd think we were in the tropics. Every couple of hours I go round swamping out red dirt and mud from our room and the public areas and the dogs help by tracking it all back again. But at least this means I can hopefully retire from cooking those hideous giant plates of mixed grill and fending off groping truck drivers in the kitchen.

CHAPTER 21

April 2012: Journey To Possession 3

Merced To Blythe

Our usual early start today - finally in sunshine. We follow Highway 99 – not the interstate this time. The difference in terms of quality and condition of the road surface is very evident. Interstates are federally funded and generally seem to be in good shape. Regular state highways rely on their own state funding and the shortfalls in terms of potholes and rough patches of surface badly in need of repair take their toll on drivers and passengers.

There are some nasty, lengthy bone-shaking sections. The recession has certainly taken its toll here, and as Governor Schwarzenegger (nicknamed The Governator after his Terminator movies) has pointed out – his state is broke. So the secondary roads can certainly do with some good ole American fixin'.

We continue south through Fresno and Visalia. Beyond Bakersfield we climb once again, this time through the Tehachapi pass with its summit at over 4000 feet. The lush green hills are dotted with rounded outcrops of sandy rock clusters, at this time of year looking so "arranged" they have an almost hyped-up enhanced appearance like a landscape in an interactive Wii game. The whole area looks groomed, yet is completely natural.

Then it's another descent, this time down to the flat expanses of the Mojave Desert. As we head east towards Barstow, we pass the Edwards Air Force Base – famed landing base of the space shuttle flights, named for the test pilot Edwards, killed while testing the Flying Wing back in 1948. The hard-packed sand surface of this part of the Mojave has provided an ideal landing area for the many return journeys of the work-horse space vehicles.

Along this section of the highway we pass intriguing, image-conjuring road signs: NEXT RIGHT: ROCKET SITE ROAD; and further on : TWENTY MULE TEAM ROAD NEXT EXIT. A lot of fabulous history behind these road signs. How did people ever make it across these barren expanses? It's challenging enough with modern highways and the assurance of a small town or rest stop within an hour or so of driving. Looking through the car windows, there seems to be nothing within sight – just endless stretches of highway cutting a swath across the desert landscape.

Somewhere out there, once stood the Mojave Desert phone booth, until its removal in 2000, to the dismay of its fans (there was even a movie made about it). Apparently it was originally put there to avail volcanic cinder miners of contact with the outside world. Fans would call on the off-chance that some lone drifter or tourist would answer. One regular caller claimed to be in touch with the Almighty via the  phone booth. God only knows how he came to terms with its removal!

Rest Stop Oasis

Barstow is at a major intersection in the middle of all this nowhere-nothingness. It is an oasis of gas stations, a Subway, convenience stores and restrooms. It is jam-packed with semi trailer trucks, motorhomes spewing out tribes of children, grandparents, and pets; bikers, and cars packed to the rafters with travel stuff, and roof racks accommodating the overflow. This is the kind of place where you really see America on the move.

A first impression might be one of chaos – but it really isn't. Everything is organized, and everyone seems to obey the unspoken rules of etiquette – waiting your turn, helping with information. We're all in this together, in the middle of the desert, and without goodwill and cooperation we know we're not going to make it back to civilization and easy access to all the creature comforts we've come to take for granted.

After a sandwich and coffee we press onward to San Bernardino and into the Coachella Valley and other popular snowbird destinations like Palm Springs, Indio, Desert Hot Springs and Bermuda Dunes.

Windpower Gone Mad

Suddenly an amazing sight emerges before us. As far as we can see down the desert valley floor there are windmills, hundreds of them. It looks like something from a sci-fi futuristic movie. It's extreme environmentalism – the Green Movement on steroids! This can't be good for the planet any more than can the scary nuclear option.

Each windmill is huge when you get up close and cosy with it. From a distance a few might look quaint, but on this massive scale the impact on the topography, flora and fauna of the desert must be appalling. Just thinking about the damage from huge trucks and machinery being driven in to haul the component parts and set them in place makes any claims about not leaving a footprint totally ridiculous. This whole valley has become one oversized stomping ground! And for what? Do the figures really justify this environmental carnage?

Sceptics claim that the blades are limited in their function to winds that are not too strong. If there is insufficient wind, the mills shut down and revert to electricity; if the winds are too strong, the same applies. And one estimate puts their production at about 5% of the electricity actually needed. We wonder if the whole enterprise is not some kind of Green fundamentalism. Somebody is making a fortune making wind turbines, that's for sure. On this scale I can't believe they are truly a part of the green movement – something's out of whack here.

The underlying problem that no one likes to talk about is, of course, population – there are simply too many of us on the planet, needing power for our homes and gadgets. Idealism aside, something has to give, and it looks like it's the environment. Too bad for the reptiles and coyotes – sorry fellas.

Back in British Columbia, with the ever-increasing encroachment of housing developments into forests and mountain habitats, bears have actually started breaking into homes and raiding the refrigerators! In one family's garden a mule deer took on the guard dog and kicked the bijeezuz out of it, score: Bambi 1, Guard Dog 0. From the point of view of the animals (if they're allowed to have one) it must seem grossly unfair when the animal control people show up with tranquilizer darts and haul off the animals rather than the humans!

The Accidental Sea

Distractions now, as we approach Palm Springs, passing signs to Bob Hope Drive and Gene Autry Trail. We enjoy a nostalgic moment or two as we see the Salton Sea signposted off to the southeast, an amazing and unnatural phenomenon we visited out of curiosity probably a couple of decades ago.

The Sea is actually a lake that was formed by accident back in 1905 when the folks settling in the region were digging an irrigation canal to redirect water from the Colorado River. Things were going fine until someone thought an extra few inches of width were necessary and the pickaxe wielders gave it their best.

Within minutes water was rushing in at an overwhelming rate, flooding the whole area, cascading into the natural basin --- they had inadvertently redirected the river with devastating results. Farms and mining settlements were drowned; lives were lost, and it took *two years* to stop the raging flow of water into the geological depression of the Salton basin.

Like the Dead Sea in the Middle East, the Salton Sea lies below actual sea level and is shallow and saline. Once seen as a potential tourist destination, it is now a desolate landmark, but nonetheless a haven for many bird species and their attendant human birdwatchers (*"Did you see the yellow stripe under its chin?"*).

Next we see signs to Joshua Tree National Park, another place of happy memories from many years ago. Like the Salton Sea, it lies on the infamous San Andreas earthquake fault line, and was hit by a nasty quake (7.1) in 1992, followed by no fewer than 23 aftershocks.

Although the village sits in constant jeopardy of future devastation, the residents continue to stoically offer tourist accommodations and services.

A word of warning : Couples seeking a romantic getaway in the town of Joshua Tree may be getting more than they bargain for when they say they feel the earth move!

The major towns and turnoffs peter out and then we see a sign telling us that there are no further services for some 68 miles. The road continues flat, forever. Over to our left we see the large swath of golden desert sand that is part of the Mojave. The greenery of tumbleweed and Joshua trees extends right to its edge and then stops abruptly. In the far distance where the mountains skirt the desert, we see the green belt start up again. In between it's one helluva big beach!

Desert Centre.....or What?

A wind gets up and dust devils – miniature tornados – accompany us alongside the highway. Suddenly there is a dust cloud directly ahead of us, blocking out sun, sky and visibility. We slow down to a crawl, keeping our eyes on the faint red glow of the tail-lights on the semi-trailer in front of us. Then as quickly as it hit us, the sand twister disappears, skipping out over the desert, and the road is clear again, though the surface is covered with a thin layer in the wake of the brief storm.

A road sign emerges, indicating Desert Centre at the next exit. We decide to have a quick break and top up with gas and so take the exit ramp. With no warning at all, we find ourselves bouncing along on a dirt track that seems to head off into the desolate wilds. We swing around and see what looks like an old gas station and restaurant. The gas pumps are derelict. Can't tell if the restaurant is functioning or just a skeletal ruin – it reminds us of a Robert Altman kind of movie, *Come Back to the Five and Dime Jimmy Dean* maybe? Feels a bit weird.

We return to the highway, wondering why the place warranted such a serious road sign. Later we learn that Desert Center has indeed been a real place, a small town a ways down a side road. The US Census listed the population as 204 back in 2010. However, the dirt track just beyond the road sign looked pretty abandoned, along with the gas station and restaurant. It seems to have been a good candidate for another desert ghost town. Best not to take a chance on being trapped in an episode of *The Twilight Zone!* In any case, we'll make it to Blythe with some gas to spare, and will fill up when we get there.

Blythe is the last California town before we cross the Colorado River into Arizona tomorrow. When we arrive we fill up with gas, find a motel with a Thai restaurant nearby, and crash for the night. Phoenix is only two or three hours away so we don't need to get up at the crack of dawn in the morning; we should easily be there around noon.

CHAPTER 22

September – October 2011: Movin' On

Call Of The Outback

When in doubt, I turn to Smokey for spiritual guidance, for he is wise and all-knowing and knows the value of a long nap in the semi-tropical sunshine.

After a leisurely meal of roast chicken, he sits at the shower block door and calmly greets guests for half an hour or so, does a casual mouse check round the bus, then retires for the evening until four a.m. when it's time to go fightin' with Black Cat. It seems like a sensible and satisfying way to spend the day.

After consulting with both of my four-footed companions, we agree that having spent more than a month living and working at the roadhouse it's time to move on. Smokey takes a walk round the campsite to meditate on the matter. Honey, being a dog, agrees immediately with tail-thumping enthusiasm. Some people believe that cats are smarter than dogs and show more dignity around humans. They may be right, but I love them both; they keep life in balance on those days when I think the world has gone mad.

There's an amicable but inevitable farewell to Dave; it's time to go our separate, different ways – there's still so much of Western Australia I want to see and explore. I set the GPS for Exmouth; we pause for a five-hour coffee break at Minilya Roadhouse so that Smokey can meditate in the bushes along the river, then overnight at one of the stations – a great alternative to the sardine-can caravan parks.

The next day brings us to the stunning turquoise coastline of Cape Range and the Ningaloo Reef – I check in at the Yardie Creek Homestead and spend a blissful couple of weeks snorkelling with turtles, reef sharks, wrasse and hundreds of sparklingly beautiful fish.

After this, things get confusing and therefore very interesting. I head down to Carnarvon for some supplies, and the bus gearbox falls to bits. I wait at the Minilya Roadhouse for two days until Tezza can come up with the flatbed truck and take us to the garage. It's not cheap, but I'm still way ahead on the Winnebago budget – and I get to meet lots of nice people at the roadhouse as I pass the time painting the sides of the bus.

Turns out it's going to be a long wait for a new gearbox, so Tezza kindly parks my bus up at the Capricorn Caravan Park, which turns out to be brilliant – again, I could fill a book with all the people and goings-on, but suffice it to say that I end up in the permanent section for over a month and make some great friends – travelling nurses, a carpenter, mine workers, you name it.

I sit in my big sun hat, painting the bus, with a regular stream of visitors coming past to see how the work is progressing. Kids come along and make suggestions – "Make him blue!" – so I incorporate these into the design.

Weeks pass by with lovely weather, wonderful fresh fruit from the local farms, fishing, snorkelling up at Quobba, and falling asleep in my hammock. Little do I know it, but my life is about to change dramatically. It starts with some tomatoes.

A Stranger Comes A-Calling

So I step out of the bus one morning to discover a gift of bush tomatoes sitting on my table – a present from Jake, one of my trailer neighbours. We get to talking, and he takes me on a guided tour of some secret Carnarvon spots for swimming and gathering bush tucker - we're soon fast friends, and I agree to clean up his trailer in exchange for the use of his 4WD while he's away on his next mining "fly in fly out" shift.

Turns out his next gig is up at Newman, so I agree to drive up and meet him there so that we can go camping and exploring on the way back down to Carnarvon. I book Honey and Smokey in at the boarding kennel, pack the 4WD with water, food and emergency tools, and head off into the inland parts of WA - wow! It's my first real taste of the outback, and I love it. Mining trucks everywhere; I learn to use the CB radio to negotiate passing the road trains, and try not to wander off the road staring at the scenery.

I pick up Jake in the middle of nowhere and we head down what looks to me like a goat track leading off into a terrifying wilderness. But Jake is of part Aboriginal heritage; he knows how to access some of the sites restricted to Aboriginal people, sites that are miniature Edens tucked away and hidden from the prying eyes of anthropologists intent on "understanding" what is not there to be understood in the western-educated sense.

Apparently we need to gather some shells or small rocks to take along with us to leave in sacred places; he has permission from the elders to visit wherever it is he's taking me now – and it turns out to be astonishing.

Hidden by a low ridge of ironstone among huge paperbark and river gum trees is Paradise - a creek canyon so beautiful that I'm not going to tell you where it is! It is a vibrantly healthy, peaceful place, full of birds and tiny fish,

131

pools to swim in, and clusters of huge prehistoric palm trees.

One of the things we had to do before we crossed the creek was to "blow the water". You scoop up a mouthful of the creek water and blow it out, which is a symbolic gesture showing that you come with good intentions to enjoy and belong to the place.

The other interesting thing Jake does is an aboriginal ritual required of some places where, if you take anything, you have to leave something behind, for example if you wanted to collect a pretty rock or souvenir, you have to leave some other small object behind; he always carries shells from Carnarvon for this, so we each put a shell in the creek - just in case.

Once we had performed the water blowing ritual and taken a moment to silently extend our well wishes to the creek spirits, we followed the track that zig-zags across the creek for miles, then camped right next to the water, swimming and exploring.

As nightfall crept its way across the sky, the full moon came out and we couldn't sleep so we sat up drinking coffee and watching the night sky, listening to the gentle sounds of the water bubbling along. In the morning I walked along the middle of the creek for a couple of hours while Jake took the 4WD further along the track, setting up a picnic spot; magic. There was no one else around so we basically just ran around practically naked like feral children. Glorious freedom!

So we spend a week exploring the desert and checking out Karijini National Park, and on the way south, we stop to have a beer with some of Jake's friends in a tiny town called Meekatharra. Several days later, we are still in Meekatharra, I've fallen in love with the place, and somehow in the cheerful confusion and socialising, I discover that I've bought a house in Main Street.

After a whole lot of hilarious events, mayhem and disorganization, Jake and I end up back at Carnarvon, madly packing up the now-repaired bus, Jake's trailer, Smokey, Honey, some mice and lots of cold beer, and head back to Meekatharra - but this time, we take the inland track through the Gascoyne-Murchison region.

Sand And Lizards

The track to Meekatharra is over 600 km with no supplies en route so water is for drinking and emergencies only. We're carrying tons of water but you never know what could happen or how long it might be to wait for help. The dirt track isn't too bad but you don't know what's around the corner or whether there's a washout in the creek dips, and big dustbowl holes can appear suddenly in front of you, so you have to take it slowly. Not to mention cows and bungarras on the road, or big trucks whose dust obliterates everything in sight.

Once you leave the bitumen in Western Australia there's seriously nothing in terms of civilisation. Every dirt road turnoff has signs indicating the current road conditions and whether the roads are open or not. You check the weather forecast for the area you are heading into; it can be dry where you are, but if it's raining 500 km up the road, you could find yourself in a flash flood. The flood plains are vast and you never really know if you're on one or not. The only backup you have are the stations (ranches) which have entrances usually every hundred kms or so – in a pinch, you can drive in (though a station driveway can be up to 200 km long!) to see if they have petrol but you would only do that in a real emergency. Occasionally you might see a cattle holding-pen with a water tank and that's about it.

On our first evening we camp just beyond Gascoyne Junction, out in the bush watching thunderheads build on the far horizon. We passed a big mob of wedgetail eagles

133

eating a dead cow, such magnificent birds. I think "Wow!" every time I see them.

The clay pans where we are camped are covered with animal tracks: bungarra, big kangaroos, snakes, feral cats. The bungarra tracks are a work of art: long, even, wavy tail lines with beautifully delineated clawprints on either side. I can't resist taking a photo of a dead one we found lying at the road side, a victim of road kill.

Honey and Smokey will be locked up in the bus tonight; there's always the chance of dingos and wild dogs. Honey is turning into a bit of a wild dog herself; she spent ages burying a bone about 25 metres from our camp, then guarding it until bed time. She used her snout to push up a big pile of dirt over the bone and got really worked up whenever we pretended to walk in that direction.

Amazingly, Jake's trailer is still in one piece although I am still favoring the odds of its being nothing more than a steel frame with bits of shredded matchstick wood and terrified mice clinging to the remains by the time we get to Meekatharra. We've still got a long way to go. No matter how well you stash everything away, the corrugated road shakes everything to hell.

Jake somehow produced a mouthwatering roast beef meal complete with gravy and damper using just a cast iron camp pot and a fire; it's wonderful sitting out under the stars watching the dry lightning in the distance. We were both really tired from all the mad packing and well-wishing visitors back at the trailer park so it was an early night.

CHAPTER 23

April 2012: Journey To Possession 4

Hola Mesa!

Mistakenly thinking Arizona is in a different time zone or has possibly already switched to summertime leaving us an hour short, we get up only slightly later than we have done on the previous three days and head east. Very quickly we cross the bridge over the Colorado and are in Arizona.

We notice an interesting phenomenon in the desert landscape. Where, on the California side of the river, the predominant plant feature was the Joshua yucca trees, here on the Arizona side we have instead the Saguaro cactus. There is no sign of either one on their non-designated side of the river. It's almost as though the finger of the Creator has drawn a "line in the sand", the river being the metaphorical line, creating two quite different plant topographies. Amazing that neither species seems to have jumped the river – at least not at this point.

We start to see the hills and mountain ranges, familiar from our earlier flight to Phoenix, and now viewed from a ground perspective. After an hour or so of driving, way off in the distance we spot the hump shape of Camelback Mountain, and then we are in the midst of mega traffic as the highway adds more lanes for the increasing density of vehicles heading into the city.

The Garmin GPS does its job directing us into the lanes we need and telling us which exit is coming up. We reach the city outskirts and are doing fine until the GPS does not respond quickly enough on an exit ramp that suddenly forks north and south. There's too much traffic behind us to change lanes so we stay on the north (wrong) ramp and resign ourselves to an unscheduled mini tour of ramps, exits and entry lanes around the city.

At one point we come to an intersection with the name of a road we recognize – and we actually know whereabouts we are, but we're facing the wrong direction and are trapped into further circlings and recalculations on the part of the eternally patient-sounding female voice of the Garmin. Damn! At this point we're inclined to smash it with a hammer as payback......."*Recalcula..............*" BAM!

We lose a good twenty minutes on this merry-go-round before getting onto the right highway, and then we know the exit we have to watch out for. It comes up right on cue, and from there it's a piece of cake getting onto the avenue that takes us straight to Sunrise Acres. Because we had set our watches an hour ahead in anticipation of what has turned out to be a non-existent time change, we arrive an hour earlier than anticipated. It is just after 11 a.m. Oh well.

The gate host greets us and opens the gate. We drive down the main avenue, turn right, and then left into "our" street. We have made our first trip to what will hopefully be our winter home! Eureka!

Little House In The Urban Desert

And there it is – our little home in the land of sunshine, sitting waiting for its new owners. This will be the first time we have really had a good look at it, inside and out. We slide open the glass door and find the keys laid out on the kitchen table as promised by Bill and Joan. The place appears neat and tidy; the furniture is as well-worn as we remember it, and we determine that top priority must be given to getting rid of it along with the dead, plush carpet and linoleum tile that have long passed their "use by" dates.

Overall, the place is pretty much as we remember it from our nanosecond walk through two months ago. We unload the car and dump everything in the living room area while we decide where to put things.

Since we have arrived early in the day, we first make a trip to the bank to order cheque books, and as the bank is located inside the supermarket we do some grocery shopping to tie us over the next few days until we get into a routine. Then it's back to the trailer where we first make a move on the cupboards and drawers to see what we have inherited.

A substantial amount of stuff that needs clearing out, that's what. We start by hauling out piles of hoarded, empty margarine tubs, boxes full of more boxes, boxes full of empty coffee tins, plastic containers of all shapes and sizes (what were they saved and used for??), several skillets and frying pans that were once non-stick but have now lost their cooking surfaces, old mini appliances whose parts start falling off when you pick them up, several electric clocks with long-dead batteries that don't work even when you give them new ones, a non-working flashlight that looks like something discovered in an archaeological dig. Amazing stuff.

We fill trash bag after trash bag, gradually exposing shelves and emptying drawers that provide homes for the new stuff we have brought with us. It's a mega cleaning job as we go along, but it gradually gets done and we're having fun doing it.

The Shed

The shed is another major undertaking and we start working on it just to give ourselves extra space for storing our luggage and sports equipment. It's a good size with lots of potential. We have noticed that some people convert them into a mini extra bedroom for the occasional guest, finishing the interior with drywall, fake ceiling, nice light fixture and some kind of bed – bunk or folding. We later notice, while perusing the Yellow Pages for something entirely different, that people have taken advantage of this niche and started some very creative shed businesses: Shed Beds is one example.

Most sheds here are like ours and come with a washer and drier. Ours has obviously never had any kind of upgrade in its eighteen years of life, though what looks suspiciously like the top tier of a bunk bed has been used for storing all kinds of equipment related to the house itself.

A dusty, mysterious rotting old swatch of quilted fabric showers us with its dust as we pull it down off the bed/shelf. We have no idea what its purpose is or was. Original bedding? A dust cover of some kind? For what? Don't know – but like the old furniture, all we do know is that it has to go. It looks like something left over from the Great Plague, possibly riddled with disease and potential death – so out it goes. If it's something we find is needed later on, we'll get a new one.

Next we find a set of insect screens for all the windows – they look and fit okay, so we clean them off and put them on the windows. There's also a set of silver aluminum reflector panels that we have seen people setting up in their windows when they are leaving for the summer. The ones in our shed look rather the worse for wear, but we figure they might just do the job. For now we can leave them stacked on the bunk shelf.

Two clothes lines have been strung up in the shed, and there's a bag of clothespins. They stay. The homemade workbench and wooden drawers will have to wait for now – a quick check tells us that absolutely nothing has ever been thrown away since the original owners moved in. Later....later.

We manage to get our own stuff comfortably accommodated, with cupboards to spare – these little places are incredibly efficiently designed. What we thought were glass-door cabinets turn out to be cupboard doors with a mirrored panel on the inside. The mirrors reflect light and give an illusion of the rooms being bigger than they really are – a clever strategy.

Things now start to move quickly. We want to get a Lift&Stor bed but we can't do that until the flooring has been taken care of. The bed is an ingenious idea for small spaces - an excellent time-out space for naughty children too, maybe??

It operates on a sort of hydraulic system. The platform on which the mattress sits, is easily raised a few inches and then lifts under its own momentum. The "lid" opens and reveals all the space that mostly goes unused under a normal bed. There is a ton of room for suitcases, sports gear and whatever else needs putting out of sight.

Richard Abbey and his wife Jennifer who run the Lift&Stor shop in Mesa, are very helpful. They will make the bed and deliver it as soon as the floors are done. Fantastic service that we're just not used to.

They ask us if we need a new mattress, and we tell them "No thanks," but say we shall have a box spring and bed frame that will need to be removed. They say that will be taken care of because their business donates unwanted beds to a local charity. This prompts us to ask if they can help us get rid of the existing living room and dining area furniture. They give us the name and number of a local church that will be happy to come and take whatever we do not want. We hope (and pray, of course) that this will not evolve into the exercise in frustration we have become accustomed to back home in Canada. Time, no doubt, will tell.

CHAPTER 24

October 2011: Gascoyne Junction – Mount Gould

An Unwanted Detour

Today's leg was from just outside of Gascoyne Junction to Landor Creek, a simple 150 km stretch if you don't accidentally miss the turnoff the way I did because a certain other driver assumed I knew which turnoff to take and didn't wait which meant a scenic detour of about 250 km towards Mullewa ("Where Dirt Meets Nothing in the Middle of Nowhere").

Anyway, apart from some extremely unpleasant slithery bulldust sections I backtracked and found Jake on his way out to find me ("Babe where are you?" "Um. Near a tree and some rocks?" "Can you see a big white rock?" "No. There's a cow." Etc). Thank heaven I did the paranoid over-organizing thing and brought twice as much spare diesel fuel as I thought I'd need.

I saw lots of BIG bungarras (goannas). They have very poor eyesight. I had to keep stopping so as not to run them over and they would sit there three feet away looking around going "Hmm. What's that noise? Oh! A bus!" So, not the most alert lizard in the handbag shop if you know what I mean.

That's one big lizard!!

The only other vehicles I saw all day were some road crew who cheerfully waved and laughed at Waggin' Trail's cow skull. Honey travelled with Jake while Smokey patiently put up with the rattling and the dust in the bus (dust is just a permanent thing here, it gets in everywhere), his paws grimly clutching the corners of the desk.

Mount Gould – Crime Capital Of Nowhere

We stopped at the Mount Gould Lockup for lunch, and then decided to camp overnight. The lockup is just one of many puzzling phenomena you come across in the desert outback of Australia, bang in the middle of nowhere – like the lone Telstra phone booth out near Cue (Magoo, one of the locals, put it there, part of the great Aussie bush tradition of Putting Wacky Things Near The Side Of The Road). You also get trees hung with thongs, CD's, shirts....weird.

The great thing around Mount Gould is that you can camp anywhere – just pull up and enjoy the silence and solitude. The site is now a tourist spot where you can take photos of the cheery windowless cells and, as the convicts once did, watch the windmill creaking round and round and round and...

Apparently the jail was built in 1888 by settler pastoralists so that the police didn't have to keep walking prisoners to the jail in Carnarvon (!). I had to wonder what you could possibly find to do that's illegal out here with thousands of kilometers of empty wilderness.

Didn't see any dingoes but we heard them howling in the early morning. I got Honey singing along as well which resulted in a puzzled dingo silence before they started up again. We packed up camp after breakfast and set off for the final leg to Meekatharra.

CHAPTER 25

April 2012: The Makeover

Tally-Ho!

Furniture clear-out is the first major step. Back home in our corner of Canada, the regular charities no longer seem to do furniture pickups, and instead rely on the donor to deliver it to their stores or warehouses. Or, we will get a phone call letting us know that a truck will be in our area in a couple of weeks' or a month's time, but only to pick up clothing and small items. So we don't expect a quick fix for our current getting-rid-of-furniture situation in Mesa.

We call the church phone number that the Lift-and-Stor folks gave us. It's mid-afternoon and we anticipate having to arrange a time for them to come and pick up the stuff maybe in a few days' time. A friendly-sounding young woman answers the phone   We tell her our situation. She says they will be pleased to come and take the furniture off our hands, and then apologises because, she explains, they probably can't manage to fit it in *today*. TODAY?? We are amazed! No problem, we say, and it's arranged the church will send someone over tomorrow morning. We start to believe in divine intervention!

Promptly next day a pickup truck arrives with a crew. The person in charge is Pastor John, a portly guy probably in his forties. He supervises the three other younger guys as they pile the items onto the truck. They all seem taken with what remains of our British accents. Pastor John calls out "Tallyho!" as each item is hauled up, and one of the younger guys asks me what it's like having to switch to driving on the right-hand side of the road in America. I explain that we emigrated to Canada more than fifty years ago, so we're kind of used to it by now.

When all is loaded, Pastor John comes over and asks if we have anywhere to go for Easter (it will be Easter Sunday this coming weekend) and hands us a couple of small flyers listing the times of the church services. We accept it for what it is - a neighbourly gesture of concern and friendliness – nobody's calling "Hallelujah" or trying to give us their god's blessing – thank heaven. So we accept his offer at face value and tell him we'll see how we're fixed for Sunday. They drive away, waving, with a final "Tallyho".

No Hablo Espagnol

The house is pretty empty now. We bring in a couple of patio chairs to sit on, and eat outside at the patio table. Time to start making enquiries about flooring and getting estimates. So at 6 p.m. the guy from the flooring company turns up, quickly checks out our floor area and tells us they will contact us next morning. They do. Just before 10 a.m. we receive the phone call. Again, we're expecting a completion time frame of probably a couple of weeks.

"If you would like to come into the store right now and choose the laminate, we can start on the job today and finish it tomorrow," we are told. Incredible! We jump in the car and drive out to Apache Junction to choose the laminate.

The warehouse outlet is a magical wonderland of house construction materials – beautiful mosaics, stone bath fixtures, wonderful styles of wash basins, panelling, wrought iron, natural stone fountains – it's enough to make you want to start all over and be in the trades that know how to shape and install these wonderful materials.

There is a wide range of laminate flooring to choose from, but we limit our choice to those that are in stock rather than having to wait for weeks on a special order. We choose a dark maple that appeals immediately to both of us.

While we're making our selection, the subcontractor and crew are being summoned and soon arrive in the parking lot. They are American-Mexican. Juan, the supervisor, is fluent in English and Spanish. The three fellows who will be doing the work speak only Spanish.

We are furious with ourselves for not keeping up with our Spanish. We got lazy after attending a party back home where everyone told us we didn't need to bother with the language because "....everyone in Arizona speaks English regardless." Talk about being ethnocentric!

Well folks, it ain't so. It's fine being linguistically arrogant if your travels only ever take you to protected enclaves and carefully planned tours that ensure your monolingualism will never be challenged. However, it seems only polite to us, that we make at least some basic effort whenever we find ourselves in regions with more than English available. The fact that all notices, road signs, services and businesses in the Mesa area seem to be in both English and Spanish should tell you something.

So now here we are, with our *tres amigos*, relying heavily on hand gestures, a sort of international game of charades, and much use of *"No hablo Espagnol muy bien."*

As they attack the job at hand, Peter and I sit outside at the patio table, me with my iPod and ear buds, tuned into *In-flight Spanish,* desperately trying to recall vocabulary and the minimal grammar this programme offers.

We've used this language series before, mostly as a basic rote memory tool. The blurb on the DVD jacket implies that if you listen to the programme a few times while you're sitting on an aircraft travelling several hours to a destination, upon arrival in the new country, you are good to go conversing suavely with the locals.

Of course, there's not much grammar-teaching in this kind of programme, so although you know how to say "I like tacos", you're rendered speechless when you find yourself trying to say, "*We* like tacos." Little things like that leave us resorting to the old backup, *"No hablo Espagnol"* or pointing to a brilliant little picture book we found decades ago in a small travel shop. It has clear pictures of absolutely everything – tools, food, clothing, transportation – everything – *todos*! BUT – we haven't brought it with us on this trip, so we're all heavily dependent on goodwill and acting ability.

The trio get down to work straight away. They work for hours and only take one short break to eat their lunch. Yet they remain cheerful and polite throughout the hot day. We manage to retrieve a tin of peanuts, a packet of raisins and an apple each from the kitchen before they head back in and get back down to work.

The hours go by. We keep thinking they'll quit for the day. Five, six and seven o'clock tick by. Around 6:30 p.m. we think one of them is telling us they are stopping now and will return *mañana* – with which we heartily agree: *"Si, si!"* But the work continues. Even if *they* are not starving by now, we certainly are, and so at 8 p.m. we move into major Academy Award acting mode saying, *"Finito! Muy bien!"* and *"A casa!"* miming eating and sleeping, and insisting they stop work for the day. We have never seen people work so hard!

The irony is that all round the resort park, residents put these wretched ornaments out front of their properties that are pottery take-offs of the derogatory portrayal of "lazy" Mexicans sitting with arms folded round their knees, a sombrero pulled down over their faces, snoozing. Nothing could be further from the reality we have witnessed. You have to wonder what these hard-working fellows make of them. The thing is, that if you go to the weekly mega Mexican Marketplace just down the road, there seem to be plenty of Mexican-American vendors selling the wretched things to white folk and anyone else who wants to buy them. Maybe to them it just isn't an issue as long as they are managing to make a living. Heaven knows, the Hispanic population in Arizona is under a lot of pressure right now with threats of new, drastic immigration laws looming ominously over their heads.

Anyway, we're the only people who seem bothered by it, and there's nothing we can do; and we haven't come down here to follow in the steps of Zapata and start a revolution! We're supposed to be on holiday.

The floor installation crew return on *lunes* and put in another long day. They are perfectionists. Nooks and crannies where the flooring and trim are not readily visible, like behind the fridge and under the built-in desk area – places where we would have said we didn't need to worry about the finishing – all have to be given the full treatment. It involves much measuring and tricky power-and–hand-sawing – and lots of sawdust blowing around outside. We stay out of the way.

Juan shows up to check on the crew and their progress. He inspects every bit of the work. The men stand back respectfully and await his approval. He emerges from the house smiling, and says the job is done; we are to walk through with him to double check that everything is to our satisfaction. To us it looks brilliant – perfect, giving our little house a completely new, modern look.

The two of us go into the shed as the men start cleaning off and packing up their tools and equipment. We find a couple of old brooms and are ready to clear off the sawdust and debris scattered in the carport. Juan blocks our way, and tells us. "No no. Not necessary."

Once the equipment is loaded onto their truck, the men unload their own brooms and sweep out the whole area. You would never know they had been here. They offer to hose it down but now it's our turn to say "No No. Not necessary. Is enough – *basta.*" We will do it later.

They climb into the truck, smiling. *"Adios!"*

"Adios," we call to them, *"Y muchas gracias."* Must hold our end up with a modicum of Spanish!

"De nada!" they call and, well-muscled arms waving out the windows, the truck turns the corner and is gone. Amazing people. Superb job.

A Work in Progress

After

CHAPTER 26

November 2011: Mission Accomplished

Meekatharra – ttthhankkk Ggggoddd!!

We roll into Meekatharra VERY tired of the bone-jarring dirt road and with fewer teeth than we had when we set out! Smokey never wants to get in the bus again. It has been very hot (37.6 C degrees outside and climbing – it's not even summer yet!) and he has spent a lot of time on his perch in front of the bus air conditioner. Everything is covered in red dust. Never been so glad to see bitumen in my life.

First stop: cold beer for the humans; ice creams for Honey and Smokey.

Then we plonk down under the trailer awnings at the home of our temporary abode – Johnno's house – a friend of Jake's. The bus and trailer have been pretty much reduced to rubble-on-wheels after the washboard road tracks. Not to worry. All can be fixed now that we've reached civilization (well, sort of).

The only highlight on the final leg of the journey was when Jake hit a huge bungarra that ran into the road. So as not to be wasteful, he put it in the back of his 4WD. Then at Johnno's house he cooked it in a fire pit in the backyard and roasted it up for dinner. It tasted great, sort of a cross between chicken and fish. If you have ever eaten swordfish it's a bit like that. The main thing is not to look at it until it's on the plate in non-lizard form. I'm pretty sure it won't make it onto MasterChef, but we will definitely be bringing a roasted rear leg when the Queen invites us round for the reciprocal overseas barbecue in her Jubilee year. I wonder if "We" will be amused??

PJ, the resident seven year old at Johnny's house, is fascinated by the pets although I do wonder what his prior pet experiences have been since his comments consist entirely of "We used to have a cat/dog/bird but it's dead" and "Will it eat me?" He is fascinated with the bus and comes over to inspect my bandit-and-dog painting. We had an interesting conversation………..

> Me: So, what do you think?
>
> PJ: Well, it looks kind of....awkward.
>
> Me: Awkward?
>
> PJ: I think the bandit's guns should be other way around.
>
> Me: Really? But what if he's left-handed?
>
> PJ: Hmm. Well it looks weird. Is Smokey a boy cat or a girl cat?

This was followed by an intensive examination of the bus interior and many more questions. "Can I try the toilet? Is that where you sleep? How many fans are there? What's your favourite thing in the bus? Can you swim? What does this button do? Are you married? Does Honey like the fan? Can we look at the fossils again?" He comes in and ransacks the bus every afternoon but is very good and puts everything back where he finds it.

In typical WA come-and-go style, Jake and I get bored with each other and he heads off south. I feel hugely grateful to him for seeing me safely across the desert and showing me new places and survival skills. but being an independent type, I'm also happy to be a single-woman operation once again - the whole adventure has got me addicted to freedom.

Little House in the Outback

First, and just to get it out of the way – Meekatharra is an Aboriginal word meaning "place of little water." Which makes sense in the dry months of the year (August through November). They don't seem to have a change-of-name plan for the wet season when as much as 20 inches can fall in a short period of time, causing many roads and tracks to be cut off by the accompanying floods.

The population is about 1000 people and about 27,000 dogs. Meeka is the Royal Flying Doctor Base for the midwest region, so there's a hospital. I've been slowly getting to know the town by taking on some jobs. Medical specialists like dentists etc visit about once a month so I have to remember to organise appointments in advance. I don't want to know what a mobile dental clinic consists of ("just bite down on this stick").

There's a tiny community centre where you can do banking for a couple of hours in the mornings, take driver licence tests once a month, and other services like internet and computer courses; it's really good. The post office dog is Bindy, who pops her head up behind the counter when you go in but is too short to hand you the EFT machine or weigh parcels, so Russell does it. There's an outdoor cinema (abandoned), a café (derelict) and three pubs (always busy). The busiest place in town, however, is the police station.

Now, the house. Oh my god I bought a house! It was ridiculously cheap, I'd had a few beers, it seemed like a good idea. I don't know it, but once again fate has delivered a gift beyond my wildest dreams - another adventure is about to start, even though the initial impression doesn't sound that exciting

It's what is called in Australia "a relocatable" – what Mum and Peter would call a double-wide trailer – two halves screwed together. In solid shape, needs a good clean-out, sits on a huge block of flat land on the main street with empty land blocks on either side; just needs a paint job and new floor laminate.

Right behind the house is a quartz outcrop – who knows, maybe I'll be finding giant gold nuggets in the backyard. The idea is to buy it, spiff it up, and maybe flip it and make a bit of profit. Or if the gold boom doesn't happen I can rent it out to the government workers at a healthy weekly rental (high rental demand here regardless of mining activity). But we'll see what happens. I'm always aware of the fact that at any time I might get the urge to hit the road again with a bus full of stray dogs and injured wildlife!

CHAPTER 27

April – May 2012: Keeping The Economy Going

Spend Baby, Spend

With the house devoid of all its furniture now apart from the bed mattress, it's time for Phase 2 : Buying New Stuff. Priority is given to getting the bed situation under control. We've been sleeping just on the mattress on the living room floor while the laminate was being installed. Now it's time to contact the Abbeys again at Lift&StorBeds.

Over the phone we order the new storage bed. There is a choice of finishes. We choose a maple veneer. The store will take away the old box-spring and frame, and the new bed will be delivered and set up for us next day. Right on time it arrives, and the two good-humoured guys set it up and show us how the system works.

That major item taken care of, we head off in search of furniture stores. We don't need a lot – a couch, chair, office chair for the computer nook, a couple of end tables, lamps, and a small table and two chairs for the dining nook. That should do it.

We have held onto a gift certificate someone gave us for Christmas, for a specialty store we particularly like, and that has a branch not too far away. We check out several other places first, just to see what the choice is, but return to the specialty store and buy the end tables and small dining table. There are no matching chairs for the dining table and we can't seem to agree on what we see in the store, so although we now have a table to eat off, we have nothing to sit on – we'll have to eat standing up for now.

Back home, we get our purchases assembled and set up – fortunately a simple matter of jamming A into B – no Ikea-type rocket-science assembly needed here, thank goodness. This is as much as we achieve in our one-day hunt. We had always thought that the phrase "Shop till you drop" was just an outworn expression, but – we're exhausted!

We flop down on the new bed and seem to slip into a coma! It is dark when we wake up. Too late now to do more. In any case, it's enough for one day. We're not used to the heat, and any physical effort at the moment feels like working in a deep-sea diving suit or something.

Over the next couple of days we find all the remaining furnishings we need, and our little home is looking pretty snazzy. Another week and a half finds us with a new hot-water tank to replace the original, 18-year-old existing one; new innards for the malfunctioning toilet, new faucets for the bath tub, and special tinting film for the windows. The trailer has also been given a new coat of interior paint.

The final item to replace is the rather depressing once-white curtain drapery covering the sliding glass patio door. A visit to one of the big box hardware stores takes care of that – vertical slats in a shade called Maui Sage. We have the window "treatment" professionally installed, knowing our limitations on do-it-yourself-and-destroy-your-relationship skills.

And voilà – we're done! Which just goes to show how quick and easy home improvements can be when you simply throw money at them!

Throughout the upgrading procedure we encountered an interesting aspect of American business dealings in this part of the United States. Almost every person who came to install or change whatever needed fixing, stayed for a visit after the job was finished. We'd pull out our cheque book ready to pay, and they'd say something like, "Okay. Let's deal with this and then we can visit." Then they would park themselves on one of the chairs and ask where we were from and we'd do the same with them, sharing information about families – children and grandchildren and where everyone was living and how often we all get to see our sometimes very scattered offspring.

They always left with assurances that if anything went amiss with their work or product they would put it right, for sure; and of course there was always the familiar "Welcome to Mesa" and handshakes and sometimes blessings as they waved goodbye and drove off. The effect was that we were always left feeling we had made new friends! If you're a cynic you probably see it as a clever business strategy – and maybe it is just that – but we felt the friendliness and interest were quite genuine, and it made us feel more at home, because we "knew" some people. Once again, a side of America that will not make an appearance on the headline news.

Starting To Feel Like Home

Well, there's only so long you can sit looking at a place saying, "Isn't it *nice?*" We rest up after all the shopping, cleaning, ordering, chucking out, and then it's time to start getting into some kind of new routine. The weather has turned on the heat something fierce by now, and we're thankful for a) the air conditioning, and b) the fact that in future visits we shall be here only for the cooler months – November through March.

We watch what the locals and permanent-stayers do. They get up very early to do whatever fitness and health activities they are into. Peter heads off to the gym around 7 a.m. I have been walking and lightly jogging around the whole complex shortly after that. A full circuit is just short of 2 kms. Some people do several loops to increase their distance. I'd like to get into some tennis again, but the sign-up list has been shut down for the summer. However, Peter reports seeing a group of women on one of the courts and thinks it might be an All Play. I decide to check it out.

I get my gear and go and stand by the gate to the tennis court again, and of course am invited to join the group. They look pretty good. Turns out they have all been ranked and play for The League. They ask what level I am, and I explain that I've never been ranked and so have no idea. "Just play," they say, "Don't worry about it." After a few games, they say that in November, when we return, I should put my name down to be ranked. They tell me I will be a "real asset". I'm pleased and flattered.

Like the folks I played with back in January they think I'm a good 2.5, which is the level most of them are playing at. However, Betty is a 3.5, and there are a couple of 3.0s. It shows. The games are good, and fun. They play every day except Sunday at 7:30 a.m. for a couple of hours.

Talking to Cindy one day, she tells me she had to be up early that morning in order to play at another resort park at 5:00 a.m. !! Talk about keen! I play every day, but as time passes and the heat increases, the group loses players as they begin to leave for cooler locations until the fall. It will be my turn to say goodbye soon.

I head for the pool each day after playing tennis and doing a short workout routine in the little gym. Peter and I can see that it's going to be a bit of a challenge fitting in all our activities when we come back in November. We haven't even got round to cycling and hiking this time as it's been much too hot. Then there are the mysteries of Pickleball to explore – we had never heard of or seen this game before. It seems incredibly popular.

We've got into a pretty pleasant routine by now, and everything is feeling more like our second home. We're getting to know some of the people; we know where to find the post office; Peter has discovered downtown Mesa on his way to the T'ai Chi studio. Things are starting to feel familiar.

Before we know it, our time is up – for now. We have to return to Canada and deal with the other part of our lives there. It's hard to leave our little house. We've grown to love it. The house back in Canada will seem enormous, going from 400 square feet back to 1800. It will feel quite decadent. We have already started to wonder if we shouldn't sell it and move into a trailer park somewhere in the semi-desert region of central British Columbia.

Whatever we decide, our experience with a very scaled-down mode of living in our little trailer home has substantially changed our perceptions of what we think we need in order to live comfortably. Maybe long-term trailer dwellers are smarter than they are given credit for! For now at least, we're happy to be joining their ranks.

Hasta luego Mesa!

EPILOGUES

Epilogue 1 : Meekatharra

April 1st. 2012

Exactly one year ago I was driving along the Great Ocean Road thinking OH MY GOD I SOLD THE HOUSE I SOLD THE HOUSE I'M LIVING IN A BUS OH MY GOD and wondering if each little noise heralded an impending and irreparable breakdown/explosion/fire. Sooty was curled up under the blanket in the back on her harness, Honey was perched anxiously on the pile of stuff in the passenger seat looking at me like "This is just a day trip, right?" and Smokey was lying in his zen-like lion pose gazing at the passing scenery, utterly unperturbed.

Ben, Kate and Sam saw me off amid cheerful "Oh I'll be fine!" and "It'll be a blast!" comments from me, which became OH MY GOD I SOLD THE HOUSE WHAT THE HELL AM I DOING as soon as I got around the corner ("Is that a normal noise for second gear..?").

None of it was what I expected, all of it has been amazing, and it's absolutely the best thing I've ever done. I learned to become an adventurer rather than just a tourist, scared myself silly, discovered I can do pretty much anything, and found that sometimes the best things happen when things go wrong.

Living in a little bus turned out to be easy - you discover that you really don't need a whole bunch of "stuff", and the people you meet on the road are all happy, friendly, sharing and fun - after all, they're doing what they want to do. I met nurses, signwriters, roo shooters, web designers, plumbers, carpenters, people from all walks of life who'd found a way to take their work skills on the road.   I never felt lonely or afraid - in contrast to city life, I learned to smile at strangers and welcome the unpredictable.

After some degree of chaos and missed deadlines, the deal on the Meekatharra house went through and I moved in. Much renovation has taken place in the double-wide, and the yard is big enough to accommodate Waggin' Trail and lots of my other stuff.

Following a horror-movie battle with the well-established cockroach community in the house, it is now clear of the wretched beasts, though this being the Outback, there is always something lurking and ready to move in – giant stick insects for example. But I'm coming to terms with it all. For instance I became quite fond of a huge stick insect that chose to hang out clinging to my computer screen. Where others might have resorted to a flame thrower, I let it sit there while I took photos of it. It seemed happy.

Smokey and Honey have been joined by Ethel the chicken, and they all get along. So far nobody has eaten anyone else! "Boy", an abused dog I adopted and rehabilitated briefly, had a happy life with us too for a while. He *loved* the bus (I would find him sitting in the driver's seat, just waiting for the next ride) but was unable to control his urge to get out of the yard and run into the middle of the highway where he would stand barking at oncoming road trains. He did it one time too many and was killed outright when one of the huge trucks hit him. I buried him in his own special place in the back garden, wrapped in his favourite blanket.

There was no further news of Sooty.

Meeka continues to grow on me, even with all its shortcomings. I now write articles for the local newspaper – the Meekatharra Dust – work part-time at the elder hostel for the local Aboriginal people, and have joined the volunteer fire and rescue brigade. Our local joke is that the fire brigade helped me by donating a dog, some chooks and a bloke - one of the volunteers sent his mate Gary around to pick me up for a blind date, and we haven't been apart since.

Unlike city life, we feel we are an important part of this place, making a contribution, enjoying the day to day where work and socialising merge - no one has to "catch up for a coffee" here, and our lives are not separate from work. It's a good feeling; it feels right. We have our vegie patch, chickens and cosy hearth, but there are also ghost towns, secret canyons, kangaroos, emus and a vast, starry sky - we don't have to go on holiday, or "get away from it all", because it's here, a place where the colours and landscape continue to feed my soul.

Perhaps one day I'll publish the full adventures of Waggin' Trail - but for now I'm happy to sit outside with Smokey, gazing at the endless sunset horizon and agreeing with him in silent contemplation that home can be anywhere, anywhere at all.

Epilogue 2: Mesa

August 2012

The return journey to Canada from Arizona was three days of jaw-dropping landscapes again. Straight desert highways stretching into infinity; huge expanses of land with here and there a lone ranch tucked up against the barren, rolling hillsides Who lives there and what made them decide it was the perfect location for putting down roots?

We skirted Las Vegas on the highway, and wondered if it had lived up to the dreams and anticipation of the trailer lady at the Mount Shasta rest stop. Hopefully Lady Luck was in a beneficent mood.

We are spending the summer travelling round the warm semi-desert interior region of British Columbia, looking for a place to live that might replicate, as closely as possible, the climate of Mesa during the Canadian summers. Our house back on the coast is going on the market, and we plan to scale down into something half the size at least. Several areas in central BC are starting to offer small, well-built manufactured homes along with mobile home parks similar to those in Mesa for seniors who still want an active life. So we'll see.

Younger folk continue to be surprised at people in their 70s still doing long distance cycling and - in Peter's case - running 10 km races. This includes one of our grown children, an expert designer-engineer of bicycle components who, when asked recently for his advice on purchasing new mountain bikes said we should not be entertaining the idea at our age because we shall be tempted to do dangerous things and end up getting injured. I suppose a couple of rocking-chairs might be seen as more age-appropriate, but it's not going to happen any time soon, we hope!

I am taking tennis lessons with a good young coach who is determined that I'll rate at least a 3.0 by the time I return to Mesa to be ranked for The League. "This is serious," he says, "None of this hit-and-giggle tennis. When you return to Mesa I want them wondering what's hit them." If nothing else, his enthusiasm is catching, and my two-handed backhand is no longer the guilt-laden experience of college days!

We shall continue to drive back and forth to our little trailer in Mesa, though at some point we'll probably switch to flying there if the three-day drive starts to be a bit too arduous. Or maybe we'll move on and try something else – who knows? Australia always beckons and we'd emigrate there if we could.

When you think about it, always playing it safe on Life's Merry Highway (which often feels like negotiating the I-5) doesn't make for much variety. I suppose we're all afraid to some extent of our inevitable end – namely dying – at least *I* am! - and staying put in one place may seduce us into thinking that that's our best option; but could it possibly be that, in fact, what we're *really* afraid of is *living*? Maybe our motto should be:

BETTER SORRY THAN SAFE!

As I write, our Canadian summer is winding down; the leaves are turning to their spectacular autumn reds and golds, and in just a few weeks it will be time to load up the car and head south again to our little trailer in the sun before the snowflakes start to fall.

The Authors

In North America:

Rhona Davies was born in England and emigrated to Canada more than fifty years ago. After a professional career, much travelling, writing, and working for two years in the Gaza Strip, she now spends half the year on the west coast of Canada, and half in Arizona, USA. Along with Peter, her psychologist partner, she writes, cycles long distances, plays lots of tennis and hopes genome research will come up with anti-aging treatments pretty soon before time runs out for both of them.

In Australia:

Anna Johnson was born in Canada and emigrated to Australia more than twenty years ago. She gave up a successful career, beachside mortgage and expensive lattés to explore her country of adoption more intimately, living in an old bus. She now has a home near a remote outback town where she works at an aged care hostel, writes for the local newspaper and lives happily with her firefighter partner Gary and the two faithful pets – Honey the dog, and Smokey the cat – who accompanied her on her odyssey.

18933776R00093

Made in the USA
Charleston, SC
28 April 2013